D A T A

01000100   01000001   01010100   01000001

(THE PRIMORDIAL AND INFINITE SWAMP)

William Houze
Weather Helm Publications
Arrowsic, ME
December 2018
ISBN: 9781731156624

Contents

Foreword

Okay, so I wrote this little book about big and not so big Data and how it might well be just another instance, among many in the primordial and infinite swamp, of what exists with no known rhyme or reason. As with everything else in the universe: it just is what it is, and that's all folks! *Q.E.D.*

Am I the proverbial old man, the crotchety contrarian who has too much time on his hands? Now that I am retired and facing another long, cold, and dark winter in the Maine woods, maybe that explains everything?

The folks quoted below[1] seem to be kindred spirits in that they share my views when it comes to data. And they will likely never see, let alone read this book. After all, it is but a single drop of datum in the sea of data that is everywhere at once in everything that ever was, is, or will be.

Here is what few have to say:

*"Data—**the final frontier**—if you have no choice in the matter, or no better place to go."- Anonymous*

"The whole enterprise of teaching managers is steeped in the ethic of data-driven analytical support. The problem is, the data is only available about the past. So the way we've taught managers to make decisions and consultants to analyze problems condemns them to taking action when it's too late."- Clayton M. Christensen, management professor at Harvard

"The problem with data is that it says a lot, but it also says nothing. 'Big data' is terrific, but it's usually thin. To understand why something is happening, we have to engage in both forensics and guess work."- Sendhil Mullainathan, Professor of economics, Harvard

"Every second of every day, our senses bring in way too much data than we can possibly process in our brains."- Peter Diamandis, Founder of the X-Prize

---

[1] https://www.springboard.com/blog/41-shareable-data-quotes/

"Data adds concrete information to a teacher's observations and intuition, but it will never replace experience, personal relationships, and cultural understanding."- Jose Ferreira, Founder and CEO of Knewton

Drum Beats from the *Data Jungle*

And these micro-vignettes depict how people relate to the data they encounter in different ways as they live their lives in our modern data-driven world.

"The first thing and last thing I do every day is look at my cell phone to see the latest dashboard metrics. I look in vain for what every CEO looks for: good and bad performance indicators that I can base action on. But all I see is the up-down of the needle; the different percentage slices of the product line sales pie; the changing quarter-over-quarter trend lines in green, amber, and red. And when I ask my CIO: 'what is it costing us to put the dashboard on my cell phone when it shows me nothing that I can make any decisions on?" he shrugs and says, 'we are doing what our competitors do: mining the truth from Big Data.'" (Jerome Stuyvesant, CEO, Millennials for Millennials, Inc., NY, NY)

"I monitor the tolerance readings on the 3D milling CNC machines. I know by the real-time operational log data of the machine's performance against set parameters and programmed tolerances when to intervene. I take it offline, run all the normal diagnostics programming to overwrite and recalibrate it, run three complete cycle tests to compare the output against our QC tolerance requirements. If it all checks out, it goes back online in limited capacity until it proves out. This is how I use CNC programming and historical and real-time output data to ensure the outcome is what is expected and acceptable to our most important customers: Boeing, GE, and Rolls Royce. (Jason Chenoix, Mechanical Engineer, Ajax Aerospace Manufacturing, Torrance, CA)

"Last Tuesday we noticed what we suspect is big-time-order-of-magnitude data corruption. We brought in Dr. Singh and Legal right away. Dr. Singh said for starters to explore checksum mismatches in the disk drives, and to be on the lookout for high spatial and temporal locality correlations. He also mentioned to analyze for identity discrepancies and parity inconsistencies. Thank god they were handed off to Martha's team since I know checksum well, but the other two not so much. Legal looked worried, took lots of notes, but said nothing in the meeting." (Larry Sudlow, Principal Software Engineer, Data MuOnics, West Roxbury, MA)

"Gross negligence by Qwerty Data Management and Consulting, LLC to detect and remedy rampant silent data corruption in the Cloud was the kiss of death for my client's database, and as a result it cost them tens of millions of dollars in lost revenue until the new system could be put in place, tested, and certified as safe upon which to run their business. Settlement in favor of the plaintiff for 158 million dollars is pending final review by the presiding three-judge panel." (William Blackstone, Esq., Fry, Ezer, Choate, & Blackstone, LLP, Chicago, IL)

"We are always fearful of losing our data. It would mean no billings out and no revenue in. If we cannot borrow and hold off creditors until it is restored, we would be out of business within sixty days. That's what the new CFO said at our last senior management meeting." (Michael Blancerio, Director, Revenue Cycle, Christian Hospital Complex, Toledo, OH)

"Talk about vastly different data domains and the variance of how that data is used per sound scientific principles and methods. Consider the basic domain differences across these entities: NASA, Amazon, NIH, SETI, First Bank, the NFL, and Kroger's. Which follow sound scientific methodology, and which do not I leave to your contemplation." (Constantine Xinides, grad student in Cybernetics at a major New England university)

Humans are Raw and Refined Data

It is an understatement of galactic proportions to say that DATA is the *sine qua non* for the IT intelligentsia around the world. This includes IT data miners, AI decision augmenter/automation programmers, and denizens from the Land of Apache Hadoop and the like.

Show me one CIO or one CFO or one CEO who embraces data without questioning its pros and cons; without admitting that it is like a golden egg in one's hand that in a second can be nothing short of a grenade whose pin has already been pulled. The whole-hearted believer in all things data exists but is not likely to be the executive running the show. Such a person would be an anomaly akin to looking for the random muon in the outskirts of Bern.

Today, is it proper to say, albeit somewhat tongue in cheek, that one cannot do the following without data:

- Drive a new Mercedes to Eddie's Bar and Grille
- brush one's teeth
- make love to one's spouse
- give birth to a bouncing baby boy or girl
- achieve tactical advantage on the battlefield
- take a daily aspirin and vitamin
- produce the latest and greatest widget that no one really needs
- Recalibrate the geostationary orbit of a satellite
- Shuttle data via smart software from one Amazon data hub to another via the Cloud in the event of catastrophic data hub failure (aka data = business continuity)
- track the DOW without data
- fly a Cessna from Brunswick to Sanford without data
- insert a stent in an abdominal aortic aneurism

- have a proper funeral without data
- Work as a particle physicist

Data is everything and everywhere. You cannot pick up a leading IT publication (or an obscure one for that matter) without reading at least one feature article on such topics as:

- Data is all-important today and will be even more so tomorrow (whatever that really means!)
- The Enterprise cannot operate efficiently, effectively, competitively, and make money without using all kinds of data for all kinds of distinct and interrelated purposes.
- How to best capture, store, protect, mine, report out on, and analyze data in a format that can be understood and acted on by "the decision makers in charge"
- Enterprise Resource Planning (ERP) software is the engine that produces transactional data that is used to "operate and manage" the financial, production, human resources, planning, budgeting, and R&D components of business operations.
- The scope of data capture, management, governance, and usage spans a range of business activities, a few key ones being:

  - Market share and trend analysis, resource allocation
  - Production planning based on calculated demand
  - Supply chain analysis, automation re-ordering points
  - Financial reporting, budgeting, planning, and forecasting

- Human resources staffing management and turnover analysis, succession planning, recruitment
- Long- and short-term strategic planning
- Sales tracking and trend analysis
- ROI target setting and measurement analysis
- Operational reports to subject matter experts (SMEs) and management
- "What-if" scenario business modeling and analysis, followed by recommended tactical and strategic adjustments (minor and/or major) to senior management

A Few Bars of Typical Hosannas for King Data

The following titles of the following articles typify the breadth and depth of the orthodox view held by some of the incredible importance of data as the MAIN COG in the Enterprise Engine.

- The Role of Data in Business. **Chron,** *by Kimberlee Leonard; Updated October 25, 2018.* "The modern business marketplace is a data-driven environment. The role of data is to empower business leaders to make decisions based on facts, trends and statistical numbers. But with so much information out there, business leaders must be able to sift through the noise, and get the right information, so that they can make the best decisions about strategy and growth."[2]

- "Importance of Statistics to Industry & Business," **Bizfluent**, by Jim Woodruff - Updated June 28, 2018. "Business managers use statistics as an aid to make decisions in the face of uncertainty. Statistics can be used for making sales projections, financial analysis of capital expenditure projects, constructing profit projections for a new product, setting up production quantities, and making a sampling analysis to determine the quality of a product. Using statistics provides real data about complex situations rather than making decisions based on unsubstantiated hunches."[3]

- "Understanding the Importance of Data Management A Decision Maker's Guide," **Dashboard Insight – Turning Data into Knowledge**, by Lyndsay Wise, Monday, June 2, 2008. "Although executive interaction with business intelligence and performance management solutions generally involves accessing and interacting with dashboards and reports, it is still essential to understand how backend data comes

---

[2] See, https://smallbusiness.chron.com/role-data-business-20405.html

[3] See, https://bizfluent.com/about-6360783-importance-statistics-industry-business.html

together to provide the necessary ingredients to enable better decision making. In a world where business units are becoming more self-sufficient and knowledgeable about managing their overall processes through the use of technology, it becomes more important to identify the value of data and its interaction."[4]

- "The Importance of Data in Health Care," Lumdex, May 31, 2013. ""[Data-powered IT tools] are helping clinicians and patients get the latest and greatest evidence-based, life-saving best practices at their fingertips. And much more."[5]

- " How big data can revolutionize pharmaceutical R&D, By Jamie Cattell, Sastry Chilukuri, and Michael Levy, **McKinsey and Company**, April 2013. "After transforming customer-facing functions such as sales and marketing, big data is extending its reach to other parts of the enterprise. In research and development, for example, big data and analytics are being adopted across industries, including pharmaceuticals."[6]

- "How Does the Military Use Big Data?" **Emergency Management, DHS,** by Colin Wood, January 6, 2014. "Collecting, correlating and making sense of big data into a single, cohesive image is called creating a common operating picture (COP). Another problem with creating a useful COP, Little pointed out, is that oftentimes the most valuable information isn't found anywhere in military intelligence files -- it's in the expert's head. The expert's experience,

---

[4] See, http://www.dashboardinsight.com/articles/new-concepts-in-business-intelligence/understanding-the-importance-of-data-management.aspx

[5] See, https://www.lumedx.com/the-importance-of-data-in-health-care-.aspx

[6] See, https://www.mckinsey.com/industries/pharmaceuticals-and-medical-products/our-insights/how-big-data-can-revolutionize-pharmaceutical-r-and-d

knowledge and intuition often play a key role in how data is filtered and interpreted to create a COP. With big data tools, however, it's possible to put the expert's knowledge into the software so everyone can use it . . .."[7]

---

[7] See, http://www.govtech.com/em/safety/Military-Use-Big-Data.html

That my view, stated below, is one that >99% of all people in the "data business" will disagree with, is a foregone conclusion.

The same will apply to vendors who push data solutions, tools, presentation layers/modes and all the various doo-dads that make up the dash-smorgasbords of data artifacts; and then of course there are the "bootcamp" entrepreneurs and the more formal and very formal and proper—don't you know--schools of computer and data science who are devoted to studying the nature, care, feeding, and grooming of the untamable creatures whose ecosystem is the digital realm that I too uncharitably perhaps call **the Primordial and Infinite Swamp**.

Data is just that – data in the database, you think--or is it?

Data has been around since the Big Bang. Data was recognized, manipulated, and at many levels understood by thinking men and women in the sciences, in mathematics, and in philosophy down through the ages.

From the birth of the scientific method (±1600 BCE), data was subjected to empirical analysis, testing, verification, and strictly limited in its use in terms of meaning of **dare**, Latin for "to give, present, what is given— (the main forms being: Do, Dare, Dedi, Datus)."

Think Euclidean proofs in plain and solid geometry, where it is "given that this follows that," which is the logical progression and orderly presentation of reasoning from the axiom to the proposition or theorem, e.g., the Pythagorean theorem.

Well and good in the evolving realm of abstract and applied Empiricism: data was understood, manageable, and used according to strict rules; inferences were based on those rules and were subjected to the scientific rigors of proof by replication and objective recording of results until all doubt about the data used in the experiments resulted in concurrence that the data was proved out.

It is having the data used in one's experiments replicated by others who use the same and then different but similar data to prove that the findings that result from the experiment are provable again and again. That the result is always the same, that it the data on the output end of the process is the same and is therefore "true" in terms of what is expected and intended to result from following the steps of the experiment to the letter.

I am not alone in this view, but it is a very different story today in the world of data as it is used—or misused-- in and by the "Enterprise."

Think Big Data. Think roughly 2.5 quintillion bytes of new data added to the massive volume already created and digitized since the digital computerization of data began in the late 1950s.

"The total amount of data in the world was 4.4 zettabytes in 2013. That is set to rise steeply to 44 zettabytes by 2020. To put that in perspective, one zettabyte is equivalent to 44 trillion gigabytes. This sharp rise in data will be driven by rapidly growing daily production of data. But how much data is produced everyday today? 2.5 Exabytes."[8]

Think layers of programming needed to "manage, store, mine, and present" big data for human review, for machine review. Think complexity and vastness on a scale that no human can

---

[8] https://www.northeastern.edu/levelblog/2016/05/13/how-much-data-produced-every-day/

grasp in practical terms, in a way that fosters positive action based on sound assumptions, on empirical structures that produced "a proof" that was accepted as truth by scientists from the Greeks to the scientists of today.

But business men and women, the Chiefs in Charge of the Enterprise, they are not trained scientists. By training and background, they are not at home in the world of modern day Data.

They rely on those who apparently thrive in that world. They hire and listen to those who form the "Data Chain of Custody and Governance" made up of teams of data caretakers who themselves have become more and more overwhelmed by the volume, complexity, and human-errors that are at the base of the data pyramid.

That base of human error—machine error is always human error—can lead to problems so deep and unfathomable that even the best programmers, data engineers, data scientists, and data theoreticians cannot come up with methods that prevent data corruption on massive and extremely costly scales.

This short book explores some of the reasons why it is now more than ever axiomatic: **live by data, die by data, for it is the primordial and infinite swamp.**

Data Basics

The Big Bang Data Matrix

Everything in the Universe, right down to the smallest "things" in matter—quarks and electrons—are data points. (As for data making up anti-matter and dark matter, you will have to check with others on that one, although it would seem to extend by definition there too.)

Even the smallest matter—think Planck length[9]--if (and when) it is defined and quantified by physicists, would be also be points of data.

The Inorganic Data Matrix

An example of inorganic matter would be pure water, air, minerals, and metals.[10] Think of the Origins of the Universe of Inorganic Data, aka the Big Data Bang, as being the matrix for what we now place as the known inorganic elements in the Periodic Table of Elements.[11]

Below are some basic factoids concerning data—what it is and how it is meant to be formed, constructed, and governed for proper and meaningful use.

---

[9] "What Is the Smallest Thing in the Universe?", by Clara Moskowitz, **Live Science**, September 17, 2012. https://www.livescience.com/23232-smallest-ingredients-universe-physics.html

[10] See, http://www.academia.edu/28570634/The_Difference_between_organic_and_inorganic_materials

[11] https://en.wikipedia.org/wiki/Periodic_table

Put another way, what follows are highlights some of the key ideas and actions that are taken to make data meaningful and understandable to man and machine alike.

The information presented is intended to establish a common lexicon and set of definitions and meanings. I will return to many of these concepts in later portions of this book.

The Organic Genome/DNA Matrix

Darwin's *The Origin of Species* (1859) is a first-rate explanation of how organic matter processed carbon-based data-points of many types as expressed in genetic and behavioral adaptations that permitted one species to survive via evolution while others fell into the dead-end of extinction. Think of extinction as being the failure to acquire, store, retrieve, and process data as and when needed in order to live another day.

Here is an example of a data-based decision tree, wherein the data encoded in the genetics of the finch morphs into a given species' beak shape, or it does not.[12]

12

https://en.wikipedia.org/wiki/Introduction_to_evolution#/media/File:Darwin%27s_finches.jpeg

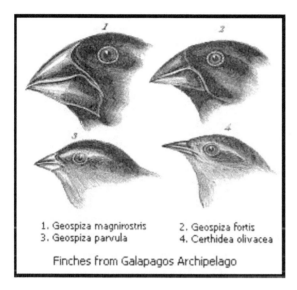

1. Geospiza magnirostris
2. Geospiza fortis
3. Geospiza parvula
4. Certhidea olivacea

Finches from Galapagos Archipelago

Homo sapiens processed data before taming fire, before learning to communicate by structured and repeated sounds, and after millennia, humans had acquired enough data manipulation skills to communicate meaning via first speech and then symbols.

(If the "data" stored in and retrieved from the brain had become corrupted, or had not been distributed to others before speech and symbology were possible, would human evolution itself have stopped? If the first one to possess a key bit of data (how to use fire? Make a flint arrowhead?) had perished before passing the data to another, would that be an example silent data loss?)

In any case, based on the work of Darwin, we have from Ernst Haeckel[13] this1910 depiction of the differentiation and selection of encoded genetic data favoring preferred traits over the

---

[13] https://en.wikipedia.org/wiki/Introduction_to_evolution

opposite. It is another example of the well-known evolution "decision tree":

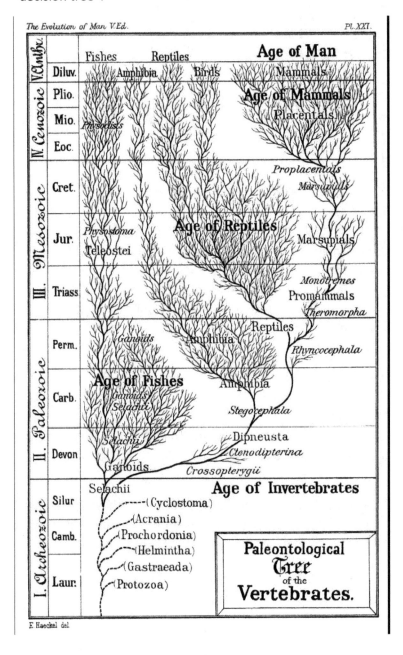

The Evolution of Man V.Ed.   Pl. XXI.

| | Age of Man |
| Diluv. Fishes Amphibia Reptiles Birds Mammals | |

Age of Man
Age of Mammals
Placentals
Proplacentals
Marsupials
Age of Reptiles
Marsupials
Monotremes
Promammals
Theromorpha
Reptiles
Rhyncocephala
Amphibia
Age of Fishes
Ganoids
Amphibia
Stegocephala
Dipneusta
Ctenodipterina
Crossopterygii
Selachii
Ganoids
Physostoma
Teleostei
Physodists
Ganoids
Selachii
Selachii
Ganoids

Age of Invertebrates
Selachii
----(Cyclostoma)
(Acrania)
(Prochordonia)
(Helmintha)
(Gastraeada)
(Protozoa)

Paleontological
Tree
of the
Vertebrates.

E. Haeckel del.

18

Here is the famous Pedigree of Man tree by Haeckel, which illustrates Darwin's **On the Origin of Species**:

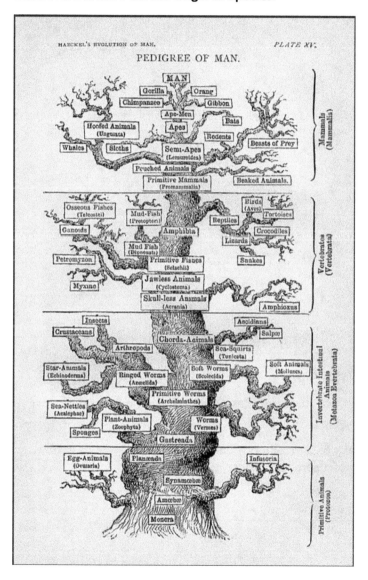

And, to bring the data decision tree concept to the present, here is one of many illustrations of the components of the human genome database[14]:

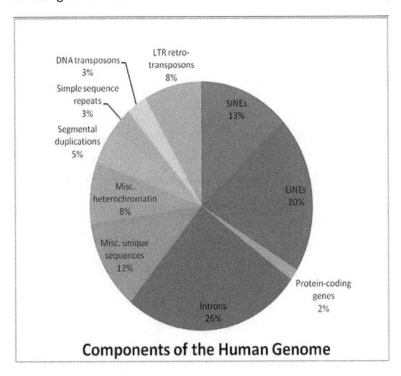

Components of the Human Genome

The Etymology: Datum/Data[15]

"Data: Mid-17th century: (as a term in philosophy): from Latin, plural of datum.

Datum: Mid-18th century: from Latin, literally 'something given', neuter past participle of *dare* 'give'.

---

[14] http://bio1510.biology.gatech.edu/module-4-genes-and-genomes/4-8-genomes/#print

[15] https://en.oxforddictionaries.com/definition/datum

Definitions from the OED

- An assumption or premise from which inferences may be drawn. *'this is not a permanent and unchangeable datum'*
- A fixed starting point of a scale or operation.
  'an accurate datum is formed by which other machining operations can be carried out'
- See also "sense datum"[16]
  - Noun: Philosophy
  - An immediate object of perception, which is not a material object; a sense impression.
  - *'the material world cannot be directly grasped via sense data or empirical observation'*
- See also "ordnance datum"[17]
  - Noun: British
  - The mean sea level as defined for Ordnance Survey.

Critical Nuanced Meaning of "Data"

Sandra Rendgen wrote an excellent article, "What do we mean by 'data'."[18] In this cogent and insightful piece, she makes several key points, which can be summarized as follows:

- Early use of data occurs in Euclid's book, "Data." The use of data in that book illustrates via geometrical axioms how something is derived from what is "given." This shows the chain of reasoning from which proposition B can be derived from the starting point A.
- "Data" as a concept and noun entity were present by the 19th century in science and statistics.

---

[16] https://en.oxforddictionaries.com/definition/sense_datum

[17] https://en.oxforddictionaries.com/definition/ordnance_datum

[18] https://idalab.de/blog/data-science/what-do-we-mean-by-data

- Empirical research produced the accepted notion that, "**. . . statisticians and scientists should observe clear rules when producing this data, to make sure it provides a reliable source of information for further study.**" (emphasis added)
- In the age of the computer ". . . the **notion that data begins to exist when it is recorded by the machine completely obscures the role that human decisions play in its creation.**" (emphasis added)

She puts her finger on the crux of the matter that is all too often ignored by those who bow before the Data Gods.

That is, data does not just exist when it is digitized and put into a computer or into the database that is accessed by the software running in the computer and accessed via humans and other machines using a given database connected computer.

Next, let's look at how data was captured and used before and after computers gave rise to "data science."

Data before computers

The answer is obvious: before computers, people used some form of writing and number system to record data that was important to them. They used file cabinets to hold the paper record of their data collected by direct observation of an activity in business, the lab, in nature, in government, on and on. With respect to the application of celestial data observations in the natural world, think Stonehenge.[19]

---

[19] https://en.wikipedia.org/wiki/History_of_the_British_Isles

And also think about the data below that many surmises were derived from and/or applied to Stonehenge by those who placed the stones in a precise manner to align with celestial bodies.[20]

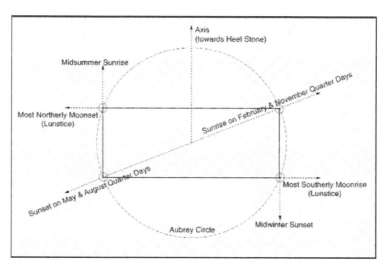

20

https://www.bing.com/images/search?q=Stonehenge+Astronomical+Alignments&qft=%2bfilterui%3alicense-L2_L3_L4&FORM=IRBPRS&=0

Fast forward to the advent of machines of various types that were used to process data before the advent of digital computers.[21]

- Teletypes
- Punched Card Machines
    - IBM 077 Collator
    - IBM 080 Sorter
    - IBM 082 Sorter
    - IBM 085 Collator
    - IBM 087 Collator
    - IBM 402/403 Accounting Machine
    - IBM 407 Accounting Machine
    - IBM 552 Interpreter
    - IBM 604 Electronic Calculator
    - IBM 029 Key punch
    - IBM 026 Key punch
- Oliver typewriter
- Monroe Monro-Matic rotary elec
- Victor
- Sunstrand manual adding machine
- Burroughs No. 9
- Microdesign (MDI) microfilm reader
- Microdesign div Bell and Howell microfilm reader
- Systron Donner Analog computer

The intersection of data and machinery would appear to be inevitable. Moving from written data recordings on paper and other media to using the abacus and then forms of mechanical and electro-mechanical devices to manipulate "information" were important steps leading to the use of computers to store,

---

21

http://www.piercefuller.com/library/hw1precomputer.html?id=hw1precomputer

manipulate, and present data as information that could be used by humans in every facet of human activity.

From the manipulation of numbers to the performance of calculations of various kinds and the storage of images on microfilm brackets the manipulation of "data" as information before the advent of the digital computer.

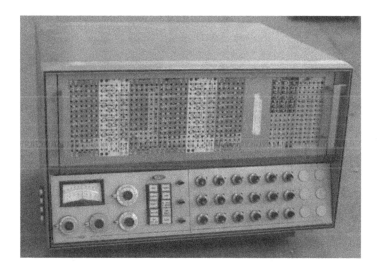

Data After Computers: The Origins of the Swamp

Taxonomy

The data can be either strictly qualitative, strictly quantitative, or some mixture of the two. The more mixed it is, the more difficult the task of making it understandable, meaningful, and actionable when presented to humans/machines. Adhering to data standards is intended to minimize data ambiguity and maximize data transparency.

Temporal Modalities

Data exists in and is presented to the "human and/or machine" consumer – i.e., data analyst/consumer/decision-maker in one of three modalities.

1. **Historical** -- in that the activity that generated the data occurred years, months, weeks, days in the past as defined as time-present;
2. **Near-real time** -- in that the activity that generated it occurred less than 24 hours ago;
3. **Historical <u>and</u> near-real time** – in that the activity that generated the data is both older than present time and as close to present time as possible.

The Data Cycle

- Created by humans/machines and transformed and/or captured by one of many machine-readable languages
- Stored in a database as an electrical quotient in a relational database
- Defined range extraction from the database via one of many logical extraction tools run by humans/machines
- Presenting,
- Understanding the Presentation

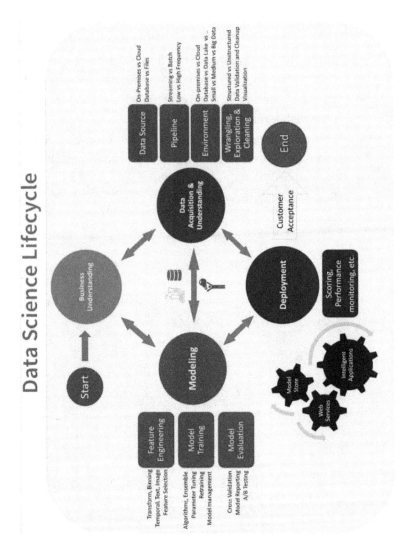

Data Science Lifecycle

Datum Health, Hygiene, and Grooming

The adage "garbage in, garbage out" (GIGO) applies to many areas of human/machine activity but is especially important in the world of data.

There are many steps along the way that a single datum takes before it reaches the datum consumer: human and/or machine.

Below are some of the major steps. The danger symbol ⚠ is in order for steps that are especially critical to establish a sound bedrock upon which the entire house of data will be built—from the small data cottage business to the mega big data mansions run by tycoons.

Like Bush 41's "thousand point of light," the big data mansions lights are burning 24/7/265. They dot the globe, and are found stacked on high in major cities, springing up in states that give them major tax breaks, or that have no state income tax (think FL or TX).

Time for an overview of the building blocks needed to unsure, if built properly, there will be consistent clarity in data construction, from the very basic elements to the more complex.

I like to think of building upon the basics as laying down key stepping stones leading up to the over-arching bridge that is erected above the data swamp. And what is in that swamp? Many things, all of them confused, confusing, a mixture that fills the morass with the Garbage in Garbage Out (GIGO) debris that all too often is the nature of data to one degree or another across and in all data domains.

Let's look at the elements from the basic to the complex. This is a brief overview of the kinds of thought processes based on standards and definitions that must be agreed upon and adhered to by those creating the data that is going to be placed in the database.

Each layer of activity, each minute step in the process can spell trouble of major consequences for those who draw upon the data when using it as the basis for making decisions that can impact the Enterprise in positive or negative ways.

Data Element Definition[22] ⚠

"A good definition is:

- **Precise** - The definition should use words that have a precise meaning. Try to avoid words that have multiple meanings or multiple word senses.
- **Concise** - The definition should use the shortest description possible that is still clear.
- **Non-circular** - The definition should not use the term you are trying to define in the definition itself. This is known as a circular definition.
- **Distinct** - The definition should differentiate a data element from other data elements. This process is called disambiguation.
- **Unencumbered** - The definition should be free of embedded rationale, functional usage, domain information, or procedural information.

"A data element definition is a required property when adding data elements to a metadata registry.

"Definitions should not refer to terms or concepts that might be misinterpreted by others or that have different meanings based on the context of a situation. Definitions should not contain acronyms that are not clearly defined or linked to other precise definitions.

"If one is creating a large number of data elements, all the definitions should be consistent with related concepts.

"Critical Data Element – Not all data elements are of equal importance or value to an organization. A key metadata

---

[22] https://en.wikipedia.org/wiki/Data_element_definition

property of an element is categorizing the data as a Critical Data Element (CDE). This categorization provides focus for data governance and data quality. ⚠

"An organization often has various sub-categories of CDEs, based on use of the data. e.g., Security Coverage – data elements that are categorized as personal health information or PHI warrant particular attention for security and access

"Marketing Department Usage – the marketing department could have a particular set of CDEs identified for identifying Unique Customer or for Campaign Management

"Finance Department Usage – the Finance department could have a different set of CDEs from Marketing. They are focused on data elements which provide measures and metrics for fiscal reporting

"Standards such as the ISO/IEC 11179 Metadata Registry specification give guidelines for creating precise data element definitions. Specifically, chapter four of the ISO/IEC 11179 metadata registry standard covers data element definition quality standards.

Using precise words ⚠

"Common words such as play or run frequently have many meanings. For example, the WordNet database documents over 57 different distinct meanings for the word "play" but only a single definition for the term dramatic play. Fewer definitions in a chosen word's dictionary entry is preferable. This minimizes misinterpretation related to a reader's context and background. The process of finding a good meaning of a word is called Word sense disambiguation. ⚠

Data Dictionary[23] ⚠

"A data dictionary, or metadata repository, as defined in the IBM Dictionary of Computing, is a 'centralized repository of information about data such as meaning, relationships to other data, origin, usage, and format'.

Oracle defines it as a collection of tables with metadata. The term can have one of several closely related meanings pertaining to databases and database management systems (DBMS):

> • A document describing a database or collection of databases

> • An integral component of a DBMS that is required to determine its structure

> • A piece of middleware that extends or supplants the native data dictionary of a DBMS."

Meta Data[24] ⚠

- **Metadata** is "data [information] that provides information about other data". Many distinct types of metadata exist:
  - descriptive metadata
  - structural metadata
  - administrative metadata
  - reference metadata
  - statistical metadata

---

[23] https://en.wikipedia.org/wiki/Data_dictionary

[24] https://en.wikipedia.org/wiki/Metadata

Standard Deviation and Data Values[25]

"In statistics, the standard deviation (SD, also represented by the lower case Greek letter sigma σ or the Latin letter s) is a measure that is used to quantify the amount of variation or dispersion of a set of data values. A low standard deviation indicates that the data points tend to be close to the mean (also called the expected value) of the set, while a high standard deviation indicates that the data points are spread out over a wider range of values."

---

[25] https://en.wikipedia.org/wiki/Standard_deviation

The Emergence of Data Science and Rise of Data Shamans

Writing in **Forbes**, May of 2013,[26] Gil Press offers a brief timeline on the emergence and refinement of the notion of "data science," which morphed into the person who hangs his or her shingle out stating, "Data Scientist for Hire." Press states at the top of his article that:

"The term "Data Science" has emerged only recently to specifically designate a new profession that is expected to make sense of the vast stores of big data. But making sense of data has a long history and has been discussed by scientists, statisticians, librarians, computer scientists and others for years."

He then lists the names of various people who have moved along the meaning of data science. The timeline starts in 1962 and ends in 2011. It makes for so-so reading, but it presents the names and the associated work product of those who wrote articles, held conferences, promoted ideas, sent out their opinions about the evolving importance of data science and, above all else, the emerging importance of the Data Scientist.

To spare the reader's all the timeline minutiae, see the "Data Science Timeline" in the Appendices.

I have included here only two events in the timeline that reference the emergence of the **Data Scientist.**

First event of many: June 2009 -- Nathan Yau in "Rise of the Data Scientist" touts how this new breed of scientist can "do it all," who can ". . . **extract information from large datasets and**

---

[26] https://www.forbes.com/sites/gilpress/2013/05/28/a-very-short-history-of-data-science/#5792117455cf

then present something of use to non-data experts . . .."
(emphasis added)

With respect to the above snippet from Nathan Yau—he presents a view that many others also present and champion to one degree or another. It is a view that pushes the notion that the data scientist (and/or the data engineer, take your pick) will be not just a new breed of scientist, but will be able to accomplish, nay, **will be expected to accomplish**, one or more of the following. (I might be exaggerating a bit in what follows, but perhaps not all that much). He or she will:

- transform the opaque, the murky, and the mysterious into the clearest actionable plans and will lay them at the feet of the executives who will take them up and experience something akin to nirvana
- like the alchemist, turn dross data into Corporate gold
- present the gleaming residue in the bottom of the witch's smelting kettle
- inform like never before the decision makers
- bring light across the dark Enterprise
- use data to tame the wilderness of government, military, health sciences, and R&D
- make clear to all who look upon it the revelation we have all been longing for
- empower the many to formulate sound tactical and strategic plans
- bring probability to assist in making decisions that they otherwise might not be made
- enable blind men to at last see the flowers of data that have been hidden from their eyes

Second event of many: June 2009 -- Troy Sadkowsky creates the data scientists' group on LinkedIn

- February 2010 – Kenneth Cukier writes in The Economist Special Report" Data, Data Everywhere ":" ... **a new kind of professional has emerged, the data scientist, who combines the skills of software programmer, statistician and storyteller/artist to extract the nuggets of gold hidden under mountains of data**." (emphasis added)

I think the data science timeline shows the trend away from empirical science; from the strict and narrow definition of what a scientist does when voluntarily bounded by the Scientific Method; a method passed down by the Greeks through the Enlightenment (c. 1685 and beyond into 18th century); a method that in the guise of scientists walked the halls of universities engaged in "modern science" as practiced in the leading academic centers; a method that began to become somewhat fuzzy and kept more and more at arms' length by the time we get to digitizing data in the Computer; a method that, for all its history and contribution to the product of science, at long last brought about the marketable and highly sought after traveler across the Swamp and into the Enterprise: the peripatetic, part alchemist, part mathematician, part hacker, part "imagineer," part visionary, part digital artist: the "data scientist."

More will be said about the role and duties of the data scientist in later sections of this book.

The Big Data Timeline

Mark van Rijmenam, in his blog, Datafloq, presents in 2006 a brief timeline of key events in the emergence of the term "Big Data.[27] Some key events and dates are:

---

[27] https://datafloq.com/read/big-data-history/239

- The use of "Data" for accounting and other purposes in agriculture and basic manufacturing dates back some 7000 years
- The term Big Data was coined by Roger Mougalas in 2005
- In 1887 Herman Hollerith invented a computing machine to organize census data
- In 1937, IBM develops system to handle data for the new Social Security System enacted under FDR
- In 1943, the data crunching machine, Colossus, developed by the Brits to break Nazi code
- In 1952, NSA spearheads cryptology throughout the Cold War era when deciphering coded signals was key
- In 1965, the US establishes the first data center for tax and fingerprint data storage
- In 1995 the first super computer is built
- In 2005, Hadoop was introduced by Yahoo, built on top of Google's MapReduce
- In 2010 Eric Schmidt states **"there were 5 exabytes of information created by the entire world between the dawn of civilization and 2003. Now that same amount is created every two days."** (emphasis added)
- In 2011 the McKinsey states that by 2018 there will be a shortage of 140.000 – 190.000 data scientists; and a shortage of 1.5 million data managers across the USA

The Data Scientist aka the Latest IT Soothsayer

We all know the famous line about how Helen of Troy's face alone was responsible for launching a thousand ships.[28]

---

[28] See, https://www.thoughtco.com/face-that-launched-a-thousand-ships-121367

Well, risking much criticism for mentioning Helen and the consulting firm, McKinsey, in the same sentence, I point out that a report by McKinsey[29] is credited by many with launching thousands of data scientist careers across the Grand Enterprise.

In the Executive Summary of the report," Big data: The next frontier for innovation, competition, and productivity," Report, McKinsey Global Institute, May 2011, by James Manyika, et al., the career launching passage reads:

"There will be a shortage of talent necessary for organizations to take advantage of big data. By 2018, the United States alone could face a shortage of 140,000 to 190,000 people with deep analytical skills as well as 1.5 million managers and analysts with the know-how to use the analysis of big data to make effective decisions."

And in the closing section of the Executive Summary to the Report, the authors point out that the Executives who run the Enterprise will have to assess the strategic value of Big Data relevant to their business. They will also need to assess the

---

[29] https://www.mckinsey.com/business-functions/digital-mckinsey/our-insights/big-data-the-next-frontier-for-innovation

ability of their IT staff to capture, manage, and make use of the data as a means to remain competitive in every sector where others are marshalling their forces to make out of big data all the advantages they possibly can. (More on this in the final section of this book.)

After data collection, all that data needs to be processed, researched, and interpreted by someone before it can be used for insights. No matter what kind of data you're talking about, that someone is usually a data scientist or a data engineer.

Data scientists are now one of the most sought after positions. A former exec at Google even went so far as to call it the "sexiest job of the 21st century".

To become a data scientist, you need a solid foundation in computer science, modeling, statistics, analytics and math. What sets them apart from traditional job titles is an understanding of business processes and an ability to communicate quality findings to both business management and IT leaders in a way that can influence how an organization approaches a business challenge and answer problems along the way.

Demand for and Role of Data Scientist

An article in *InfoWorld*, by Vivian Zhang and Chris Neimeth,[30] April 14, 2017, states that Glassdoor ranks for the second year in a row Data Scientist as the top job out of fifty ranked jobs in the tech field.

The article cites these key facts from Glassdoor and other sources about the demand for data scientists:

---

[30] https://www.infoworld.com/article/3190008/big-data/3-reasons-why-data-scientist-remains-the-top-job-in-america.html

- With a job score of 4.8 out of 5, a job satisfaction score of 4.4 out of 5, and a median base salary of $110,000, data scientist jobs came in first, followed by other technology jobs, such as data engineers and DevOps engineers.
- A quick search for data scientist jobs in the United States on LinkedIn reveals over 13,700 open positions.
- It's estimated there will be one million more computing jobs than employees to fill those computing jobs in the next ten years, according to Computer Science Zone.

The authors also offer some insight as to why there is such a shortage of qualified data scientists. Looking at the supply in 2017, they list these reasons for the shortage:

- There's a shortage of talent
- Organizations continue to face enormous challenges in organizing data
- The need for data scientists is no longer restricted to tech giants

Finally, they touch on the role of the data scientist, which I believe opens the can of worms that poses significant risk across the Enterprise in all domains where Big Data wrangling, organizing, and extraction calls for the data scientist's level of expertise:

"Business leaders are after professionals who can not only understand the numbers but also communicate their findings effectively. Because there is a still such a shortage of talent who can combine these two skillsets . . .." (emphasis added)

The requirement that the data scientist be versed in the arcana of data is a given; but being able to understand the various domains that create and use Big Data is another matter of considerable importance.

Not only will the demand for data scientists grow, but the domains will require that they be more than a little familiar with the ins and outs of the dollars and sense, the production issues, the quality control imperatives, and the human factor of employees working in the domains as well.

CFOs and CEOs will expect them to be able to talk the talk and walk the walk—a high order when we consider the diverse and overlapping domains that produce and use Big Data, as indicated by this graphic from Wikipedia.[31]

Data Science Training: Nine skills[32]

Burtch Works, writing in KDNuggets, lists nine skills that are essential for the would-be Data Scientist. I summarize the nine below:

Knowledge
1. Math and Statistics, Computer Science, Engineering In undergraduate and graduate school
2. Knowledge of and expertise in an analytical tool, i.e., SAS and/or R

Technical Skills
3. Python, Java, Perl, or C/C++.
4. Hadoop platform, Hive or Pig, Amazon S3
5. Able to work with unstructured data, e.g., social media, video feeds, or audio.
6. Ability to write and execute complex queries in SQL.

---

[31] https://en.wikipedia.org/wiki/Data
[32] https://www.kdnuggets.com/2014/11/9-must-have-skills-data-scientist.html

41

Other Skills

7. Intellectual curiosity
8. Business acumen
9. Translate and present technical findings to a non-technical team so the results are understood

Top Schools[33]

S.No.	Name of Program	Business	Computer Science	Statistics	Industrial and Systems Engineering	Mathematics
1.	MS in Data Science, Columbia University	10	15	20	-	9
2.	MS in Data Science, New York University	20	29	49	-	9
3.	MS in Computational Data Science, Carnegie Mellon University	18	1	9	-	34
4.	MS in Machine Learning, Carnegie Mellon University	-	-	-	-	-
5.	MS in Analytics, Northwestern University	5	34	49	-	17
6.	MS in Analytics, Georgia Institute of Technology	34	9	-	1	29
7.	MS in Analytics, North Carolina State University	52	48	15	-	52
8.	MS in Analytics, Texas A&M University	31	40	15	-	41
9.	MS in Business Analytics, Michigan State University	35	56	47	-	46
10.	MS in Business Analytics, University of Cincinnati	63	112	-	-	115

---

[33] https://www.analyticsvidhya.com/blog/2016/07/10-analytics-data-science-top-universities-masters-usa/

42

(Note: the US national rankings across the verticals--Business, Computer Science, Statistics, etc.--are from *US News*.)

Data Science Bootcamps

To meet the apparent demand for an endless supply of data scientists, bootcamps are available on a frequent basis in major cities around the world. Here is one such list from datasciencedojo[34]. There are many other bootcamp offerings as you might expect. They are easily found online.

Seattle Join the Waitlist	Nov 26 – 30, 2018
Austin 3 seats left at **25% off!**	Jan 28 – Feb 1, 2019
Barcelona 2 seats left at **25% off!**	Feb 25 – Mar 1, 2019
Washington DC 3 seats left at **30% off!**	Mar 25 – 29, 2019
Chicago 3 seats left at **30% off!**	Apr 22 – 26, 2019
New York 3 seats left at **30% off!**	Jun 24 – 28, 2019
Toronto 3 seats left at **30% off!**	Aug 19 – 23, 2019

---

[34] https://datasciencedojo.com/bootcamp/schedule/

Sample Bootcamp Format and Curriculum

From the same source, datasciencedojo, here is a description of the data science bootcamp format and curriculum. Instruction is offered online via webinars and five days onsite working with the instructors.

Bootcamp Format

50% Lectures + 50% Labs, Exercises, and Demos
- 10 hours of pre-bootcamp coursework
- 50 hours of in-class training
- 10 hours of (optional) post-bootcamp coursework
- Mentored Kaggle project participation

Course Outline

- Preparatory Material (via webinars)
    - Introduction to Big Data, Data Science, and Predictive Analytics
    - Introduction to Azure ML Studio
    - Fundamentals of Data Mining
    - Introduction to R Programming
    - Introduction to Amazon Machine Learning
- Fundamentals of Data Science
    - Data Exploration, Visualization, and Feature Engineering
    - Hands-On Labs: Data Exploration, Visualization, and Feature Engineering
    - Machine Learning Fundamentals
- Classification Algorithms
    - Introduction to Predictive Modeling
    - Decision Tree Learning
    - Logistic Regression
    - Naïve Bayes
    - Hands-On Lab: Building a Classifier
- Regression Algorithms
    - Linear Regression

- o   Regularized Regression Models
- o   Hands-On Lab: Building a Regression Model

It is an understatement of some magnitude to point out that Data Science has become a major online webinar and onsite bootcamp industry.

Many of the sites list the qualifications of the instructors. They range from a named resource who has worked as or with data scientists to Ph.D.'s from universities who teach and/or practice in industry and business. So, it is a mixed offering for sure, and as always, buyer beware when signing up for a bootcamp.

Beyond this, however, is the clear evidence that marketing for data scientists is alive and well as a slice of the overall data science, data analytics, and data engineering pie.

One can assume that the business world will be flooded with data scientist practitioners of varying background, qualifications, aptitude, and experience in business, industry, and in the larger discipline of data science itself.

Quality variations no doubt exist in the data science area just as they do in any discipline. Those who are hiring data scientists will do well to research the field extensively, so they can ask questions that help determine the candidates' **qualifications and experience in both technology and business.**

Fortune 500 job ads for data scientists

A quick look at DICE in November 2018 reveals a staggering number of jobs available for Data Scientists:

Data Scientist jobs

A major healthcare provider in the US is looking for a Senior Principal Data Scientist. The high-level job description reads as follows:

"Due to growth, we are looking to build out our Advanced Research and Analytics team and need a Senior Principal Data Scientist to join our team. You should be an exceptional Data Scientist with Machine Learning and Predictive Modeling experience and a passion for working with healthcare data, hands-on skills using various big-data and ML platform tools, and **proven experience delivering business impact on a portfolio of projects. This role will also require experience with analytics business development, evangelism and delivery of analytic solutions to business leaders."** ⚠ (emphasis added)

Here is another want ad blurb from a US Fortune 500 producer of breakfast foods:

Job Description

"XXX is seeking a Sr. Data Scientist to join an established and growing data science team in the Global Business Solutions shared services organization. Our team is the Data Science center-of-excellence for XXX, tasked with serving functional data science and analytics teams through the whole Fortune 500 organization. Some of our projects include demand forecasting, text classification, operational analytics, and pricing optimization.

We are looking for candidates who enjoy solving new, difficult problems, working with diverse internal business partners, and who can deliver continual improvement in both themselves and those they work with.

Job Requirements

* **Solve business problems** ⚠️
* **Develop novel ways to help business partners meet objectives utilizing cutting edge techniques and tools** ⚠️
* **Advocate and educate on the value of data driven decision making focusing on the "how and why" of solving problems** ⚠️
* Lead analytic approach within cross-functional projects
* Create exemplary analytic data products
* Utilize machine learning on the XXX Hadoop Data Lake to create repeatable, dynamic & scalable models
* **Engineer features by using your business acumen to find new ways to combine disparate data sources** ⚠️ (emphasis added)
* Share your passion for Data Science
* Curate and connect external data sets for broad enterprise-wide analytic usage ⚠️
* Identify and develop long-term data science processes, frameworks, tools, and standards
* Collaborate, coach, and learn with a growing team of experienced Data Scientists

Qualifications
* Bachelor's Degree required, MS or PhD preferred
* Bachelor's in Data Science, Computer Science, Engineering, Statistics and 5+ years' experience required OR Graduate degree in quantitative discipline and demonstrated Data Science skill set, plus 2+ years' work experience

Technical Scope
* Must have Python or R proficiency working with DataFrames
* Must have proficiency writing complex SQL queries
* Must have proficiency leveraging Machine Learning to solve problems
* e.g. Clustering, Classification, Neural Networks, Regression, Anomaly Detection, Ensemble Models
* Must have proven ability to merge and transform disparate internal + external data sets in multiple formats⚠️
* Experience with Git repositories, version control, and/or code reviews strongly preferred
* Experience with Big Data technologies desired -- Hadoop, HDFS, Hive, Impala, Spark, H20.ai
* Experience with data visualization tools desired -- Tableau, Spotfire, R Shiny, Plotly⚠️
* Experience with deploying and monitoring models desired

(Note: I have inserted the warning symbol ⚠️ at key points in the ad that was prepared by the HR department, likely in conjunction with members of the data science team to ensure the technical needs are included and stated accurately. They indicate where potential issues will arise in my view when the data scientist actually faces and interacts with the business community, the business SMEs, and most of all, the executives (CEO, President, and CFO. Perhaps even with the CIO, who may not have the background of the Data Scientist, or the graduate degrees.)

Typical salary for these positions runs from $85K to $115K for a senior data scientist, depending on the candidate's actual training and work experience. Not too shabby for a statistician who is bored with his or her work as an actuarial, or for the junior professor or instructor who would like to get a taste of the corporate life and out of the classroom for a change of pace and culture.

CEO, CIO, CFO, HR: are they q*ualified* to interview Data Shamans?

Is it a case of marketing hype having run its course from the top to the bottom of the corporate hierarchy which explains the apparent sign-off by the powers that be to bring aboard all manner of data science staff?

Assume that the business in question has a rudimentary data science resource pool. Who will interview the prospective data scientist, data engineer? Who will have the requisite background to ask the hard questions, to assess work experience as a data scientist/engineer in conjunction with the business community? Who will know what is smoke and what is not when discussing past work experience in the field?

Of course, checking references will help, but even in this case, the HR department will have to check with past business types, not just with those in the data science field.

Failure to carefully assess qualifications could well lead to the Data Science Tail Wagging the Enterprise Top Dogs: the CEO, CFO, CIO.

Data Mining, Modeling, and Predicting

Data Mining

Here is a standard definition of "data mining" from Wikipedia[35]:

"Data mining is the process of discovering patterns in large data sets involving methods at the intersection of machine learning, statistics, and database systems. Data mining is an interdisciplinary subfield of computer science with an overall goal to extract information (with intelligent methods) from a data set and transform the information into a comprehensible structure for further use. Data mining is the analysis step of the "knowledge discovery in databases" process, or KDD."

Data Modeling

Data mining is linked in practice to Data Modeling, which can be defined as:[36]

"Data modeling is a process used to define and analyze data requirements needed to support the business processes within the scope of corresponding information systems in organizations. Therefore, the process of data modeling involves professional data modelers working closely with business stakeholders, as well as potential users of the information system."

There are three kinds of data models that are built, per this same entry in Wikipedia:

---

[35] https://en.wikipedia.org/wiki/Data_mining

[36] https://en.wikipedia.org/wiki/Data_modeling

"Here are three different types of data models produced while progressing from requirements to the actual database to be used for the information system.

- **Conceptual data model**
    - o "The data requirements are initially recorded as a conceptual data model which is essentially a set of technology independent specifications about the data and is used to discuss initial requirements with the business stakeholders."
- **Logical data model**
    - o ". . . the conceptual data model is then translated into a logical data model, which documents structures of the data that can be implemented in databases. Implementation of one conceptual data model may require multiple logical data models."
- **Physical data model**
    - o "The last step in data modeling is transforming the logical data model to a physical data model that organizes the data into tables, and accounts for access, performance and storage details. **Data modeling defines not just data elements, but also their structures and the relationships between them**." (emphasis added)

Next is an illustration of how a data model might benefit the Enterprise[37]—assuming the model is constructed properly and used appropriately by knowledgeable model experts who explain the purpose, meaning, and limitations of the data model(s) to the key stakeholders in the Enterprise.

---

[37] https://en.wikipedia.org/wiki/Data_modeling

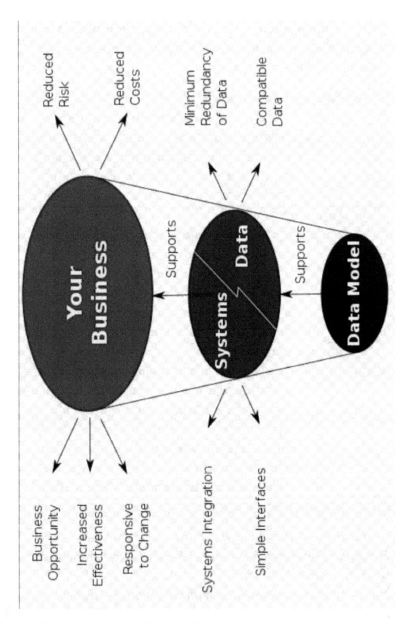

And here is a generic data model:

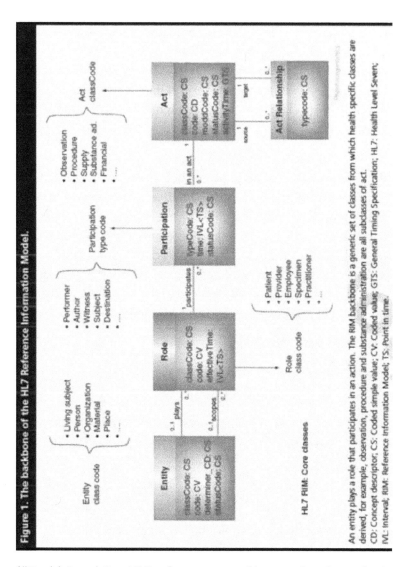

Figure 1. The backbone of the HL7 Reference Information Model.

("Health Level-7 or HL7 refers to a set of international standards for transfer of clinical and administrative data between software applications used by various healthcare providers."[38]

---

[38] http://www.hl7.org/

Clearly, data modeling is complicated and advanced work, and it calls for much training and hands-on practice before it is attempted and then presented as a viable model that can be used by a few with the background and understanding to offer out of the model information that might be of value to the Enterprise.

This level of data manipulation and structuring is not something that a set of Cloud or on-premise tools from Power BI, Tableau, or Qlik will offer the Enterprise. One thinks of the data scientist as the proper individual to perform this level of work, assisted by a team of course, who follow directions and executes assigned tasks without guessing, short-cutting, or assuming that a given activity is what is called for unless the activity has been cleared with and approved by those in the know and who are therefore in charge of the modeling project(s).

Predictive Data Modeling

The following gloss about predictive modeling is based on information found in Wikipedia:[39]

- Predictive modelling uses statistics to predict outcomes
- Most often the event one wants to predict is in the future ⚠
- Predictive modelling can be applied to any type of unknown event, regardless of when it occurred ⚠
- Depending on definitional boundaries, predictive modelling is synonymous with, or largely overlapping with, the field of machine learning
- Predictive modelling is often contrasted with causal modelling/analysis: ⚠

---

[39] https://en.wikipedia.org/wiki/Predictive_modelling

- Predictive: one may be entirely satisfied to make use of indicators of, or proxies for, the outcome of interest
- Causal modelling/analysis: one seeks to determine true cause-and-effect relationships
- Predictive "correlation is not the same as causation"

Laptop Predictive Modeling with Excel and Oracle's Crystal Ball

" Oracle Crystal Ball is the leading spreadsheet-based application for predictive modeling, forecasting, simulation, and optimization. It gives you unparalleled insight into the critical factors affecting risk. With Crystal Ball, you can make the right tactical decisions to reach your objectives and gain a competitive edge under even the most uncertain market conditions."[40]

Limits and risks of the Monte Carlo method

Here is a link to see an online demo of Crystal Ball.[41]

Based on the Monte Carlo methodology,[42] Crystal Ball is designed to work in conjunction with Excel and makes it possible to predict, for example, the likelihood of realizing a given Net Profit that derived from one or more assumed values that are entered as single deterministic values in single cells in an Excel spreadsheet.

---

[40]

https://www.oracle.com/technetwork/middleware/crystalball/overview/crystal-ball-131398.pdf

[41] https://www.oracle.com/applications/crystalball/

[42] https://en.wikipedia.org/wiki/Monte_Carlo_method

About the first step in the simulation process, Oracle has this to say:

"The first step to using Crystal Ball is to determine which model inputs are uncertain. Which values are estimates? Which are averages? Once you have identified these, you use your knowledge of the uncertainty around the input to create a probability distribution for that cell (what we call an assumption). Crystal Ball lets you define these distributions."

Admittedly, that is a lot of **emphasis added**—and for good reason!

The user would have to know how to assess uncertainty, make reliable estimates, establish averages based on knowledge of past and present activity metrics in the given subject matter or area of the business.

This is asking a lot of one or more people who are sitting on a mountain of data, which itself might well be riddled with error over the years, which then throws their "knowledge of the knowledge base" itself into question!

In any case, what we see below is the sample Oracle Excel spreadsheet. Certain values in certain cells are "known values," whereas others are "best guesses" entered by **the subject matter expert in the area of the business in question**.

In this case, let's assume it is a finance type who:

- who has intimate knowledge of how marketing plays the game
- understands the leniency management affords marketing when it comes to the budget—even if there is no written record of what is spent, when, and for what;

- is familiar with the history of marketing spend in the past—both written and not—as well as the present day realities of costs incurred by various activities in the marketing department.

So, the ASSUMED and unverified cost for marketing is entered: $16.0MM.[43]

	A	B	C	E
1		**ClearView Project**		
2				
3	Costs (in millions):			
4		Development Cost of ClearView to Date	$10.0	
5		Testing Costs	$4.0	
6		Marketing Costs	$16.0	
7		Total Costs	$30.0	
8				
9	Drug Test (sample of 100 patients):			
10		Patients Cured	100	
11		FDA Approved if 20 or More Patients Cured	TRUE	
12				
13	Market Study (in millions):			
14		Persons in U.S. with Nearsightedness Today	40.0	
15		Growth Rate of Nearsightedness	2.00%	
16		Persons with Nearsightedness After One Year	40.8	
17				
18	Gross Profit on Dosages Sold:			
19		Market Penetration	8.00%	
20		Profit Per Customer in Dollars	$12.00	
21		Gross Profit if Approved (MM)	$39.2	
22				
23		**Net Profit (MM)**	$9.2	
24				
25				
26				
27				
28				

⊮ ◂ ▸ ▸⊩ \ VISION /

---

[43] Oracle recognizes the danger at this early step in the entire chain of assumptions. Thus their product offering that is meant to bring some degree of realism to those who use Crystal Ball, or to curtail the range

Next, the finance type running this simulation would have to know the range of likely marketing costs for the given project. In this case, the ASSUMED range is from $14M to $19M for marketing costs. This range is then entered into the Crystal Ball program, which displays as shown below:

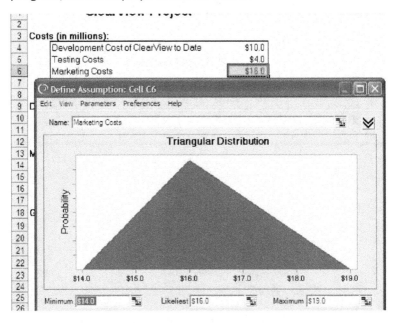

Then, pressing the button, the user kicks off the simulation logic in Crystal Ball, which runs X number of iterations of probable forecast outcomes against the ASSUMED single variable range for marketing costs.[44]

---

of assumption-making. Hedging one's bets, is another way to put it. That product is "Oracle Crystal Ball Decision Optimizer." A link to a PDF is here: https://www.oracle.com/applications/crystalball/decision-optimizer/
I
[44] See Oracle's online demo for its "Crystal Ball Decision Optimizer" product:
https://download.oracle.com/technology/products/bi/crystalball/demos/dec-opt-quick-111.html

And here is the forecast profit against the ASSUMED range of marketing costs:

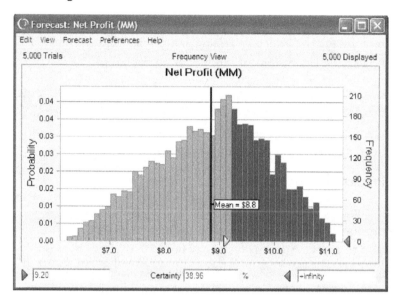

After the program runs 5000 trial iterations (which yields 5000 forecasts) against the input data, the results after the 5000 trial simulations indicates the mean profit of $8.8M. This means that the certainty of achieving the forecast net profit of $9.2MM is only 38.86%.

Who would follow the plan that would return $8.8M if they only had one chance out of three of achieving that goal? More to the point, who would base ANY strategy on the model shown, which looks at the likelihood of a **given assumption-based outcome** from a single determinant— "only one value to one cell" in the Excel spreadsheet.

Quite the reductionist approach, it would seem, one assumption about uncertainty being assessed for the probability that it will occur. Yet it is a popular modeling tool in use by thousands across the Enterprise.

For a good overview of the risks and limits of the Monte Carlo method in the financial planning and prediction area, see "The Power and Limitations of Monte Carlo Simulations,"

by David Blanchett and Wade Pfau, 8/26/14.[45] The article touts the possibility of using the Monte Carlo method in financial planning, but also makes this key point: "Like any model, you need quality inputs to get quality outputs."

Predictive Modeling Risk

Based on the foregoing brief look at Oracle's Crystal Ball product, it is redundant perhaps to ask: Is predictive modeling akin to gazing into the crystal ball but with blinders over one's eyes? Or has the "science" been advanced to the point that a high-degree of correlation exists between what is used in the model, the outcome of the model, and the reality that one sees independently of the model, i.e., the outcome occurs as predicted although the outcome was not based on human decisions that directed the course of events. It simply happened in reality as predicted by the data run through the model tool set.

And what about statistical correlations in modeling? Remember the shopworn admonishment: "there are lies, damn lies, and then there are statistics."

All of these sentiments and ideas are interrelated, and they are based on experience more often than not. They are notions that

---

[45] https://www.advisorperspectives.com/articles/2014/08/26/the-power-and-limitations-of-monte-carlo-simulations

are alive and well for good reason, not because capricious naysayers like to take shots at *data savants*.

Trying to predict what might happen in the future is possible, of course, if one does so based on empirically determined cause-and-effect actions that result from a known and analyzed given dataset. If the temperature reaches 2000 degrees F, the valve will open, and hot gas will be emitted into the chamber. When that happens, a fire will occur, and the device will be consumed in flame and will burn until nothing is left to burn. This has been observed 5,353 times and the results are always the same.

So, if I build my **causal model** on this set of conditions that are inherent in the dataset in question, I will be able to predict with a very high-degree of certainty what the effects will be.

Contract this, however, with the **correlative model** that looks for a correlation of sufficiency based on what is defined as sufficient, and if that threshold is met, then the prediction is made on that basis.

Mitigating predictive modeling/analytics RISK

This critical topic is addressed by many practitioners under the big tent Data Analytics. One, Jen DuBois, offers these pointers for avoiding risk when setting up a predictive model:[46]

- Understand the business use case (business needs and context) for which the predictive model is being created and used;

- Ensure the dataset is clean, timely, of sufficient volume, is representative, is pure and untainted by dataset contamination or unwanted mixture;

---

[46] https://strategywise.com/five-common-errors-to-avoid-when-building-predictive-models/

- Too many or too few variables
- Imbalance of bias and variance
- Model testing and evaluation errors

In conclusion, DuBois writes: "Knowing how to generate models using the latest techniques and algorithms is not enough. Analysts should collaborate with business stakeholders, track their experiments, identify and learn from modeling mistakes, and avoid them in future iterations and projects."

Big Data Predictive Modeling Failure

In "Limitations of Predictive Analytics: Lessons for Data Scientists," **DATAVERSITY**, Paramita Ghosh, June 2017,[47] the author offers this cautionary:

"The element of "surprise" is so high in Predictive Analytics that even the best of algorithms, computational models, and analytics tools can lead to complete failure in some cases. There are situations where even the best Data Scientists failed to take all the "unknown variables" into consideration, which ultimately led to incorrect data-driven predictions."

Here is another statement from another source: "12 Predictive Analytics Screw-Ups," by Robert L. Mitchell, (Computerworld (US))[48] Originally published at Computerworld

Mitchell sets it up this way:

"We asked experts at three consulting firms — Elder Research, Abbott Analytics and Prediction Impact — to describe the most

---

[47] http://www.dataversity.net/limitations-predictive-analytics-lessons-data-scientists/

[48] https://www.predictiveanalyticsworld.com/patimes/12-predictive-analytics-screw-ups/2049/

egregious business and technical mistakes they're run across based on their experiences in the field. Here is their list of 12 sure-fire ways to fail."

Mitchell's list of the 12 common predictive data modeling screw-ups, he gleaned from the three consulting firms who provided the information based on their own experiences, is a rich trove of what not to do, should have done, and could have done. The list speaks for itself, and really needs to further commentary to make the import of each of the 12 screw ups understandable for the reader. Here they are, in all their striking muddledom:

"1. Begin without the end in mind.

2. Define the project around a foundation that your data can't support.

3. Don't proceed until your data is the best it can be.

4. When reviewing data quality, don't bother to take out the garbage.

5. Use data from the future to predict the future.

6. Don't just proceed but rush the process because you know your data is perfect.

7. Start big, with a high-profile project that will rock their world.

8. Ignore the subject matter experts when building your model.

9. Just assume that the keepers of the data will be fully on board and cooperative.

10. If you build it, they will come: Don't worry about how to serve it up.

11. If the results look obvious, throw out the model.

12. Don't define clearly and precisely within the business context what the models are supposed to be doing."

All in all, a nice little list of what not to do. It is my guess that most thinking executives could come up with these kinds of no-no's themselves without ever knowing a thing about predictive data modeling. I say this because that is the way smart and successful executives think. They are all about process and taking the right process steps in the right order in the right measure and at the right time.

Let me emphasize my gloat on executives this way: **CAUTIOUS, EXPERICNCED, and SMART executives** perform as I describe. They would never make the kinds of mistakes in their daily work as attributed by the three consulting firms to data scientists who clearly are prone to go off cock-sure of themselves.

Good executives learn from their mistakes quickly and without anyone having to point them out, and if they do not, the Board takes appropriate action—in most cases one would hope. Some are fired, some are retired.

The data scientist, on the other hand, might be protected by the Data Engineer or the CIO once or twice, but after that, they should be out on their cans. This is especially likely to happen to the Ph.D. who makes the move from academe to the business world for the bigger bucks. Or for the neophyte data scientist who is getting in on the gold rush while there is still an unclaimed plot or two to stake a claim as one's own.

Data Processing and Presentation: The Business Intelligence Marketeers

BI Dollar Market Projection 2015-2021[49]

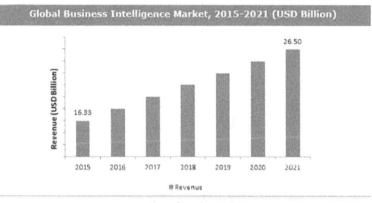

Source: Zionmarketresearch

Business Intelligence: What is it, what does it DO?[50]

"BI technologies provide historical, current and predictive views of business operations. Common functions of business intelligence technologies include reporting, online analytical processing, analytics, data mining, process mining, complex event processing, business performance management, benchmarking, text mining, predictive analytics and prescriptive analytics. BI technologies can handle large amounts of structured and sometimes unstructured data to help identify, develop and otherwise create new strategic business opportunities. They aim to allow for the easy interpretation of these big data. Identifying new opportunities and implementing

---

[49] https://financesonline.com/15-best-business-intelligence-tools-small-big-business/

[50] https://en.wikipedia.org/wiki/Business_intelligence

an effective strategy based on insights can provide businesses with a competitive market advantage and long-term stability."

Business Intelligence, 15 Best Reporting Tools[51]

What are the 15 best business intelligence tools for small and big businesses?	
1 Sisense	9 Google Analytics
2 Looker	10 Board
3 Tableau	11 Dundas BI
4 SAP Crystal Reports	12 Birst
5 Domo	13 Hevo Data
6 Microsoft Power BI	14 Rakam
7 Qlik Sense	15 Tenzo
8 IBM Cognos Analytics	

[51] https://financesonline.com/15-best-business-intelligence-tools-small-big-business/

Business Intelligence Vendor Magic Quadrant[52]

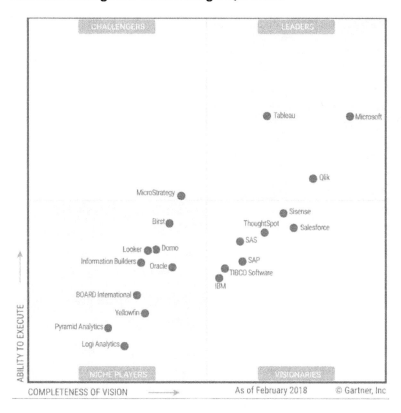

[52] https://info.microsoft.com/ww-landing-gartner-bi-analytics-mq-2018-partner-consent-test.html

What is Microsoft Power BI?

Their marketing blurb tells us that:

Power BI is a business analytics service that delivers insights to enable fast, informed decisions.

- Transform data into stunning visuals and share them with colleagues on any device.
- Visually explore and analyze data—on-premises and in the cloud—all in one view.
- Collaborate on and share customized dashboards and interactive reports.
- Scale across your organization with built-in governance and security.

For an online overview, see Power BI by Microsoft[53] which touts the product offerings as being a wonderful Cloud-based BI offering for many different kinds and levels of data miners across the Enterprise.

Power BI Product Offerings and Price levels

- Author – Free to download from Microsoft Store
  - Connect to hundreds of data sources
  - Clean and prepare data using visual tools
  - Analyze and build stunning reports with custom visualizations
  - Publish to the Power BI service
- Pro -- $9.99 per month (after 60 day free trial)
  - Build dashboards that deliver a 360-degree, real-time view of the business
  - Keep data up-to-date automatically, including on-premises sources
  - Collaborate on shared data

---

[53] https://powerbi.microsoft.com/en-us/

- o Audit and govern how data are accessed and used
- o Package content and distribute to users with apps

Power BI Pro 60-day Free Trial[54]

- Power BI Premium (Capacity pricing per node per month)[55]
  - o Share data with users inside and outside your organization without purchasing a per-user license
  - o Allocate, control, and manage your dedicated server capacity
  - o Unlock higher limits for Pro users with datasets up to 10 GB and refresh up to 48 times per day
  - o Access interactive and paginated reports online or use Power BI Report Server for on-premises reporting
  - o Deploy in the geographic region of your choice

---

[54] https://powerbi.microsoft.com/en-us/power-bi-pro/

[55] https://powerbi.microsoft.com/en-us/power-bi-premium/

Positives on above from Microsoft:

1. Empowers many in the data user community across the Enterprise
2. Offers self-service to clients and tiered pricing and levels of sophistication of BI tool set

Negatives on BI vendor offerings for BI

A few of the major negatives on above from Microsoft (or from any BI vendor offering packaged data mining and modeling software) are:

1. Assumes that the data being "mined" via tool set is clean and meets established data standards (e.g., ISO/IEC 11179)
2. Assumes user knowledge and abilities are adequate to use the BI tool set correctly
3. Places the learning curve in the hands of the users, or possibly being directed and controlled, with competency testing, via Corporate Training Department, IT Leadership, Data Officer, Data Scientist
4. Takes control of the data after initial training for users out of hands of Management/Data Scientist/Data Officer
5. Unleashes side-bar data conversations and actions across management, possibly outside of and in contradiction with the established Enterprise business rules, strategies, and other business plans that depend on collective agreement of what the data indicates in

70

the way of possible options for financial and other KPIs across the Enterprise

Microsoft has a YouTube online offering that shows many examples of data mining output as result of using Power BI.[56] Here is a pastiche of what is available in the way of dashboard data presentations:

---

[56] https://powerbi.microsoft.com/en-us/

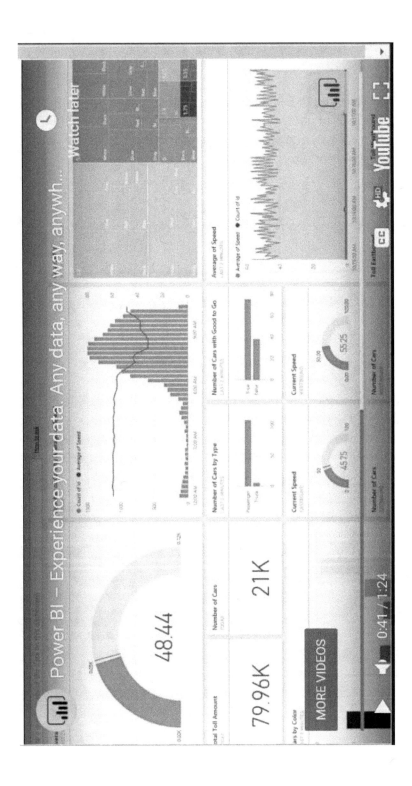

The screen below shows the user "administering and assembling the micro-data-set from the larger data set in the corporate database" in order to build reports, dashboards, graphs, and other data output.

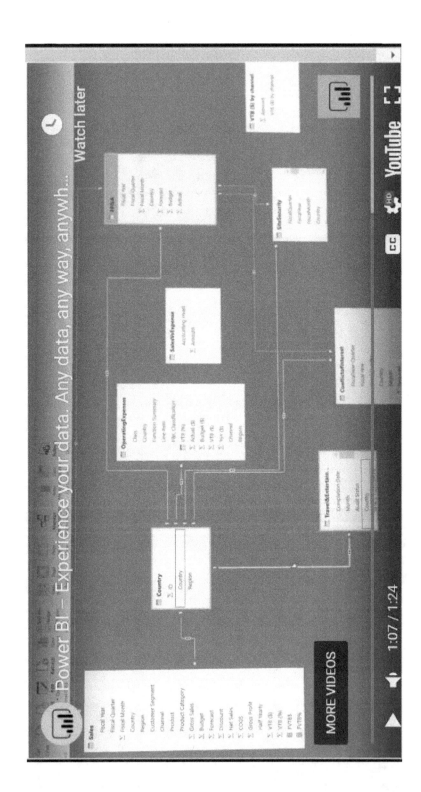

Dragging and dropping data elements and establishing data entity relationships appears to be all too easy. And it is, except that the assumption is this: the user understands the relationships that are possible within the data; and that the data itself has been built using the best guidelines so that it is clean, precise, and accurate.

Tableau and Qlik BI Offerings: A Quick Look

Gartner places Tableau and Qlik near Microsoft Power BI as the two other top BI leaders in vision and ability to execute to offer the Enterprise the "best and leading" business intelligence presentation software packages. Here is an example of the Tableau and the Qlik output from their tool sets.

First is an example of Qlik's "Executive Dashboard".[57]

---

[57] https://us-d.demo.qlik.com/QvAJAXZfc/opendoc.htm?document=qvdocs%2FExecutive%20Dashboard.qvw&host=demo11&anonymous=tr

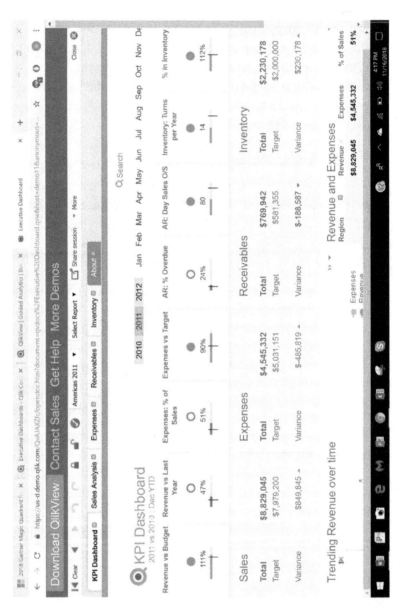

My comment on the Qlik KPI presentation is that it is information that borders on analytics visual and cognitive overload. There is so much information presented, and so many data points to digest and understand (as well as the data point interrelationships) that I wonder if the average Executive will be able to make much out of the information presented. What does the data picture say? What actions would be called for? This is especially the case if the person reviewing the data cycles through the years available; they would need to take notes to compare year over year values. A graph might summarize that, but then the elements making up each year's graph lines would be hidden from the viewer.

Given enough time to study the presentation, I assume any intelligent reader would eventually be able to come away with some key points of information, but that would take time for sure.

The demo screen online from Qlik makes it clear that the tool is very easy to use. That in itself is a benefit. But again, the data overload is a potential negative. Finally, the Qlik "presentation" software is a prime example of "data mining."

Here is a second Qlik screen for the same source company, this time showing the data for Receivables for Europe.

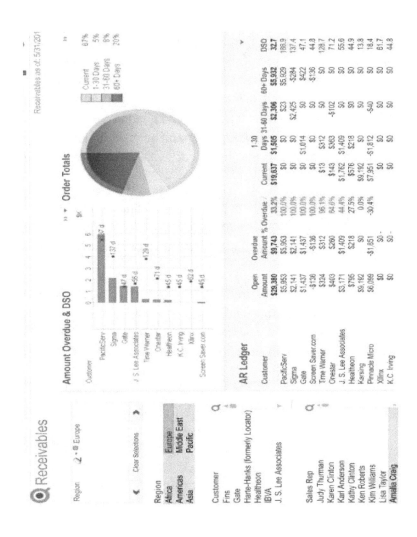

Tableau's product offerings

Tableau's product line includes:[58]

- Tableau desktop

---

[58] https://www.tableau.com/products/new-features

- o Answer questions at the speed of thought
- Tableau server
  - o Governed self-service analytics at scale.
- Tableau online
  - o Self-service analytics in the Cloud
- Tableau prep
  - o Combine, shape, and clean your data for analysis

Below is an example from the online sales promotional site by that high-lights the highly-automated and visually- based tool set manipulation by the trained user of Tableau[59]:

---

[59] https://www.tableau.com/

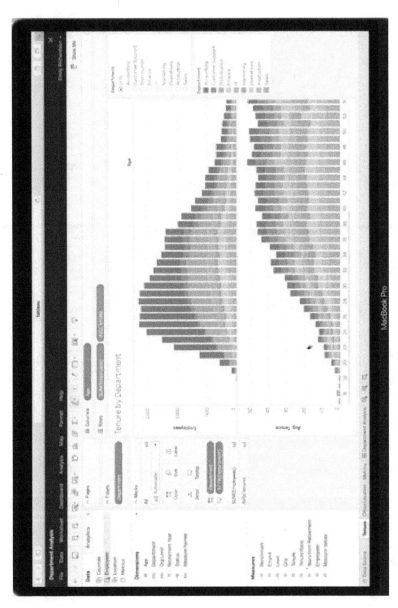

And here are two more examples of data presentations from Tableau:

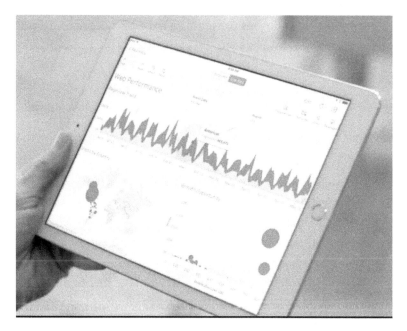

Tablet view

Conference Room screen view

A recent article in **Forbes** presents an excellent overview of the state of Business Intelligence (BI) utilization in the Enterprise.[60]

Summary key points in the article are:

- Executive Management, Operations, and Sales are the three primary roles driving Business Intelligence (BI) adoption in 2018.
- Dashboards, reporting, end-user self-service, advanced visualization, and data warehousing are the top five most important technologies and initiatives strategic to BI in 2018.
- Small organizations with up to 100 employees have the highest rate of BI penetration or adoption in 2018.
- Organizations successful with analytics and BI apps define success in business results, while unsuccessful organizations concentrate on adoption rate first.
- 50% of vendors offer perpetual on-premises licensing in 2018, a notable decline over 2017. The number of vendors offering subscription licensing continues to grow for both on-premises and public cloud models.
- Fewer than 15% of respondent organizations have a Chief Data Officer, and only about 10% have a Chief Analytics Officer today."

A Few Final Observations

These vendors offer very powerful BI tools for the user who has been trained in their use. While much of the software is visually-based and highly intuitive after the first few routines have been practiced, there remains the same fundamental underlying

---

[60] "The State of Business Intelligence, 2018," Forbes, by Louis Columbus, June 8, 2018.
https://www.forbes.com/sites/louiscolumbus/2018/06/08/the-state-of-business-intelligence-2018/#1c67080b7828

questions and assumptions that pertain to all data, however it is used, whoever uses it:

1. What is the underlying quality of the data?
2. Who has "certified" that the data is clean and is in the form and to the level that is needed by the user community, regardless of the top-end or front-end BI tool set being used to manipulate the data into reports and dashboards?
3. Who is sharing what data, with whom, and what is their authority to "act" on the data before them?
4. What policies are in place that control the employees who, while empowered by these kinds of BI tool sets, might share the data widely and propose actions on it without the knowledge of or approval of middle and senior management, right to the Executive levels?
5. Do these BI tools give the users a false sense of understanding of the various micro and macro forces external to the Enterprise that bear upon it daily and are therefore outside of the decisions that can be made based on the data sets within the Enterprise? Or even to external data sets linked to the Enterprise database (e.g., US State and Federal government statistics, Global statistics, private research firms, e.g., Gartner)?

Big Daddy-O Data

Big data images of all kinds are easy to find online.[61]

Here are two that depict the meaning of big data and how business might make use of big data.

---

[61] https://goo.gl/images/Ly63uX

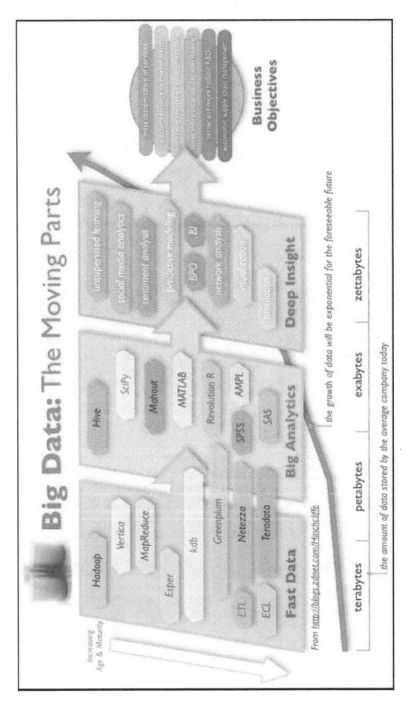

Big Data: The Moving Parts

From http://blogs.zdnet.com/Hinchcliffe

Here is a working definition of Big Data

"Big data is a term used to refer to data sets that are too large or complex for traditional data-processing application software to adequately deal with."[62]

One tool set that is commonly used to manipulate big data is Apache Hadoop, that dates back to the "Google File System" paper that was published in 2003:

"Apache Hadoop (/həˈduːp/) is a collection of open-source software utilities that facilitate using a network of many computers to solve problems involving massive amounts of data and computation. It provides a software framework for distributed storage and processing of big data using the MapReduce programming model."[63]

For a visual depiction of the emergence of Big Data, see Winshittle.[64]

Here is a nice graphic that depicts the Global Data Storage Capacity before and after the advent of the "Digital Age"[65]:

---

[62] https://en.wikipedia.org/wiki/Big_data

[63] https://en.wikipedia.org/wiki/Apache_Hadoop

[64] https://www.winshuttle.com/big-data-timeline/

[65]
https://en.wikipedia.org/wiki/Big_data#/media/File:Hilbert_InfoGrowth.png

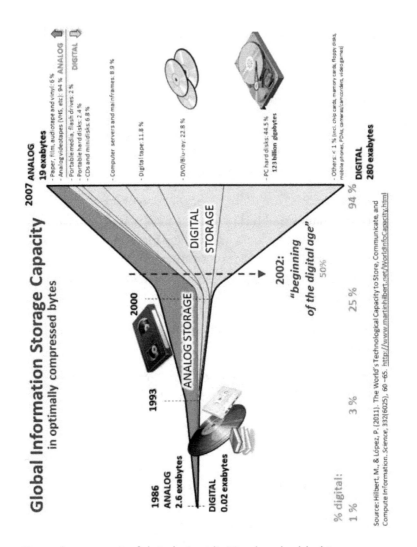

Global Information Storage Capacity
in optimally compressed bytes

1986
ANALOG
2.6 exabytes

DIGITAL
0.02 exabytes

1993

2000

ANALOG STORAGE

DIGITAL STORAGE

2002:
"beginning
of the digital age"
50%

2007 ANALOG
19 exabytes

- Paper, film, audiotape and vinyl: 6 %
- Analog videotapes (VHS, etc): 94 % ANALOG
- Portable media, flash drives: 2 % DIGITAL
- Portable hard disks: 2.4 %
- CDs and minidisks: 6.8 %

- Computer servers and mainframes: 8.9 %

- Digital tape: 11.8 %

- DVD/Blu-ray: 22.8 %

- PC hard disks: 44.5 %
  123 billion gigabytes

- Others: < 1 % (incl. chip cards, memory cards, floppy disks, mobile phones, PDAs, cameras/camcorders, video games)

DIGITAL
280 exabytes

% digital:
1 %   3 %   25 %   94 %

Source: Hilbert, M. & López, P. (2011). The World's Technological Capacity to Store, Communicate, and Compute Information. Science, 332(6025), 60 –65. http://www.martinhilbert.net/WorldInfoCapacity.html

Given the amount of data being digitized and added to databases of all kinds from many vendors, it will soon become necessary to arbitrarily limit the size and kind of data that will be used by the Enterprise and others.

Already the size and complexity of some databases is such that users access it via AI and algorithms running against the target database(s) to help the computer system mine the data "on its

88

own," which is a shorthand definition of Machine Learning (ML). And as a result, it is postulated, the humans interested in the results will then be able to "learn" about the "deep meaning" of the data set(s) in question.

The advent of truly big data is one reason that AI and

That is, "Machine learning (ML) is a field of artificial intelligence that uses statistical techniques to give computer systems the ability to "learn" (e.g., progressively improve performance on a specific task) from data, without being explicitly programmed."[66]

ML typically involves one or more of the following activities/goals as established by the data gurus who are steeped in AI, statistics, mathematics, linguistics, learning theory, epistemology, branches of philosophy, and a host of related subjects all of which are far beyond the kenning of 99.9% of the employees who want data output they can use across the Enterprise.

Here is the list, with selected breakouts to show the levels and range of arcane opened up by those who make a living pursuing meaningful creatures as they explore the depths and bayous of the data swamp:

- Problems
  - Classification
  - Clustering Regression
  - Anomaly detection
  - AutoML
  - Association rules
  - Reinforcement learning
  - Structured prediction

---

[66] https://en.wikipedia.org/wiki/Machine_learning

- o Feature engineering
- o Feature learning
- o Online learning
- o Semi-supervised learning
- o Unsupervised learning
- o Learning to rank
- o Grammar induction
- Supervised learning (classification • regression)
- Clustering
- Dimensionality reduction
- Structured prediction
- Anomaly detection
- Artificial neural networks
- Reinforcement learning
- Theory
  - o Bias-variance dilemma
  - o Computational learning theory
  - o Empirical risk minimization
  - o Occam learning
    - ▪ In computational learning theory, Occam learning is a model of algorithmic learning where the objective of the learner is to output a succinct representation of received training data.
  - o PAC learning
  - o Statistical learning
  - o VC theory

Everyone is not on board the Big Data train, of course. One website illustrates the thinking that the Big Data train is heading for a wreck of major proportions, and the passengers will be, well, less than wholesome beings as a result. Here are some of the comments posted at the end of the article, "Why is Big Data so Dangerous?[67] The blog was written by Bernard Marr. He makes several key points in his article that focuses on the major risks posed by Big Data:

- It will challenge how businesses are run and the business models that will help them succeed.
- Everything can be tracked and analyzed
- Privacy problems and discrimination become rampant
- Data about us could be used to spy on us
- finally, there is the danger from hacking and cyber crime

In response to Marr's blog posting, several readers made interesting comments (and they are all practitioners in the industry known as Big Data Buckaroos). Here are three comments of note:

1. Comment by Tony Lange on September 15, 2016 at 7:43pm "What about the danger of making false conclusions i.e. mixing up correlation with causality? Or over generalizing. I am seeing this happening by the bucketful, with the assumption the more the merrier?"
2. Comment by Boris Shmagin on September 18, 2016 at 4:35pm "There is a book: "Weapons of Math Destruction How Big Data Increases Inequality and Threatens Democracy" by Cathy O'Neil. Crown, 2016. 272 pp"
3. Comment by Dorothy Hewitt-Sanchez on September 15, 2016 at 2:36pm "I am like you passionate about Big Data; but I do see the current and future troubles. It is terrifying. Nevertheless, I think it is out of our hands. We are like drunk people driving forward 5, 10, 15

---

[67] https://www.datasciencecentral.com/profiles/blogs/why-is-big-data-so-dangerous

miles; Then suddenly we hit the brakes and drive backward 30 miles. We keep repeating the cycle over and over again. We are drunken people in the car laughing and driving. Drink a little more laughing, move forward 10 miles, stop drink a little more, put the car in reverse drive backward 20 miles, laughing all the way. Over and over again, losing ground between every stop; How far have we traveled?"

Writing in Project Syndicate, Carlo Ratti and Dirk Helbing offer this interesting gloss on the importance of keeping Big Data, AI, and much of that ilk in check so that "distributed non-machine intelligence" can work its magic as it always has over the course of human advancement in all areas of endeavor. In short, they point out the dangers of Big Data and Big AI; they avow the merits of the human penchant for daydreaming, for using intuition, for recognizing what is good in serendipitous thinking and discovery:

"But with centralized algorithms coming to manage every facet of society, data-driven technocracy is threatening to overwhelm innovation and democracy. This outcome should be avoided at all costs. Decentralized decision-making is crucial for the enrichment of society. Data-driven optimization, conversely, derives solutions from a predetermined paradigm, which, in its current form, often excludes the transformational or counterintuitive ideas that propel humanity forward."[68]

And here are three final examples from individuals who see in Big Data (and the algorithms needed to mine the data) more harm than good in its progression in the hands of people who

---

[68] https://www.project-syndicate.org/commentary/data-optimization-danger-by-carlo-ratti-and-dirk-helbing-2016-08

might well have good intentions but who are incapable of managing the genie once out of the bottle.

- "Big data is like nuclear technology. It could be used for constructive uses as well as destructive uses. The similarity lies in its ability to cause more harm than good."[69]
- And on the inevitable bias humans build into their algorithms, here is food for thought from **Inside BIGDATA -- Your Source for Machine Learning**: "It's tempting to regard algorithms as objective, unbiased constructs that are free from the corruptive influence of human prejudices and biases. Unfortunately, this is seldom the case. Because algorithms are designed by humans – and increasingly learn by observing human behavior – they tend to adopt the biases of their developers and of society as a whole."[70]
- From **Experfy**,[71] these important points on Big Data risks are made:
  - "Privacy/Security: The biggest risk that anyone familiar with big data knows is privacy concerns and security issues that emerge from such concerns.
  - Deriving conclusions from erroneous data patterns:
    - Huge datasets have two severe limitations: 1) They evoke "false confidence" in the predictive capability of analysts. 2) Results from Big data

---

[69] https://electronicspost.com/dangers-of-big-data/

[70] https://insidebigdata.com/2018/07/16/dangers-algorithmic-bias/

[71] https://www.experfy.com/blog/major-hurdles-big-data-risks-threats

analytics can be easily manipulated, misinterpreted, or misused by individuals or organizations to present a strong case in their favor.

- o Limitations of big data: Big data, no doubt, has the capability to provide "decision-makers with more timely, rich information," but without a deep understanding of the associated context, analysts will fail to relate the data to the story."

Below is Gartner's summary from 2018 of how AI is beginning to be used to facilitate decision-making.[72] Talk about a nice depiction of what I believe will be a very slippery slope:

" Decision automation systems use AI to automate tasks or optimize business processes. They are particularly helpful in tasks such as translating voice to text and vice versa, processing handwritten forms or images, and classifying other rich data content not readily accessible to conventional systems. **As unstructured data and ambiguity are the staple of the corporate world, decision automation — as it matures — will bring tremendous business value to organizations.** ⚠️For now, decision automation accounts for just 2 percent of the global AI-derived business value in 2018, but it will grow to 16 percent by 2022." (emphasis and warning symbol added)

Deep Trust (or Distrust) in Data-Chain-of-Events Reality

The data in the base storage bin gets there via a series of events, often referred to as what happens from start to finish of the Data Life Cycle, which falls under the rubric of Data Science lifecycle. Here is one sowing 7-steps in the data science life cycle:[73]

---

[72] See, https://www.gartner.com/newsroom/id/3872933

[73] There are hundreds of data science lifecycle depictions in the public domain on the Internet. See,
https://www.bing.com/images/search?q=Life+Cycle+Science+Project+Data&FORM=IDINTS

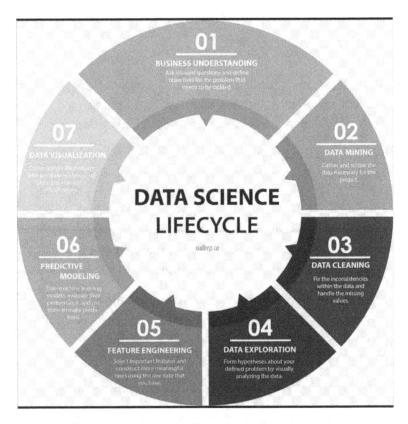

It goes without saying but I will say it: each step presents a myriad of potential issues, misunderstandings, failures to execute per expectations, so forth. At best it is an iterative process that if done as carefully as possible might produce choices and recommendations for further consideration. But there is to my way of thinking just way too much risk throughout. A key mistake at any one of the steps along the way could well produce what is discussed below.

GIGO: "Garbage In, Gospel Out"

In 1988, Paul Watzlawick made a very key statement. He wrote:

"Garbage in, gospel out" is a more recent expansion of the acronym. It is a sardonic comment on the tendency to put excessive trust in "computerized" data, and on the propensity for individuals to blindly accept what the computer says. Since the data entered into the computer is then processed by the computer, people who do not understand the processes in question, tend to believe the data they see and take it just as seriously as if the data were Gospels.[74]

Vagaries of Data Interpretation

Data Quality[75]

Data quality refers to the condition a set of values of qualitative or quantitative variables. There are many definitions of data quality, but data is generally considered high quality if it is "fit for [its] intended uses in operations, decision making and planning".

Alternatively, data is deemed of high quality if it correctly represents the real-world construct to which it refers. Furthermore, apart from these definitions, as data volume increases, the question of internal data consistency becomes significant, regardless of fitness for use for any particular external purpose. People's views on data quality can often disagree, even when discussing the same set of data used for the same purpose. Data cleansing may be required in order to ensure data quality."

Three Responses to the Data Gods

---

[74] See, https://en.wikipedia.org/wiki/Garbage_in,_garbage_out; taken from this source quoted in Wikipedia: Paul Watzlawick (1988). Aldri så godt at det ikke er galt for noe [Von schlechten des Guten oder Hekates Losungen] (in Norwegian). Translated by Kjell Olaf Jensen. [Oslo]: Ex Libris. p. 78. ISBN 8273841367.

[75] https://en.wikipedia.org/wiki/Data_quality

Data Believers -- They are "all in."

They have paid their money and want to believe at all costs. They also do not want to seem behind the times, or blind to what everyone else claims to be as obvious as the nose on your face.

Data Agnostics

They are ambivalent, which means sometimes they act on what is presented, sometimes they do not—there is no rhyme or reason for the response to what the investment in data presentation machinery

Data Atheists – They are Likely Unemployed

They invited in the leading vendors, they attended the presentations and the demos, they asked all the right questions, they were skeptical going in, and skeptical coming out, they did not take the leap of faith needed to commit the time, capital, and other kinds of investments in technology to move forward.

Instead, they continued to rely on time-based financial data, sales performance data, and what is in the news in terms of competition, new comers, promising technologies that might have a short mid or long term impact on the market in question.

Analyzing Data: What Does It Tell You and What Does it Mean?[76]

Interpret the Results

"Once you've organized your results and run them through whatever statistical or other analysis you've planned for, it's time to figure out what they mean for your

---

[76] https://ctb.ku.edu/en/table-of-contents/evaluate/evaluate-community-interventions/collect-analyze-data/main

evaluation. Probably the most common question that evaluation research is directed toward is whether the program being evaluated works or makes a difference. In research terms, that often translates to 'What were the effects of the independent variable (the program, intervention, etc.) on the dependent variable(s) (the behavior, conditions, or other factors it was meant to change)?'"

"There are a number of possible answers to this question:

- *Your program had exactly the effects on the dependent variable(s) you expected and hoped it would.*
- *Your program had no effect.*
- *Your program had a negative effect.*
- *Your program had the affects you hoped for and other effects as well.*
    - These effects might be *positive.*
    - These effects might be *neutral.*
    - These effects might be *negative.*
    - These effects might be *multiple*, or *mixed.*"

Data Analysis – Common Errors and Omissions

Data Presentations

There are many ways to present data:

- Analog and digital dials (real-time metrics)
    - Data telemetry (aerospace, medicine, manufacturing, power grids, etc.)

This data display is prone to error of course, if the data feed source is itself sending incorrect data. However, the advantage of this kind of presentation is that it is immediate, near-real-time, and is more easily understood once the viewer is trained what to look for and to assess the meaning(s) rapidly of what is presented—aka quick validation assessments.

- Reports (online, paper, desktop, etc.)

Reports are by their nature historical or recent presentations of data. They are meant to be read and analyzed. They rely on the reader's familiarity with the content, the context of the data presentation, and the ability of the reader to assess and determine the meaning of what is presented in text and graphs, and other images that convey data relationships over time, volume, dollars lost/gained, etc.

- Management and Executive Dashboards

These data presentations are perhaps the most *au currant* at this time. They are also prone to as much misinformation as the analog dial and the report data mediums of presentation. They can also mislead because the data presented is primarily graphical in nature (pie charts, X-Y graphs, color trend lines, etc.)

Data validation[77]

"In computer science, data validation is the process of ensuring data have undergone data cleansing to ensure they have data quality, that is, that they are both correct and useful. It uses routines, often called "validation rules," "validation constraints," or "check routines", that check for correctness, meaningfulness, and security of data that are input to the system. The rules may be implemented through the automated

---

[77] https://en.wikipedia.org/wiki/Data_validation

facilities of a data dictionary, or by the inclusion of explicit application program validation logic." ⚠️

It is hard to imagine a step in the entire chain of data use events more important than this one: data validation. Again, the rules, constraints, and routines need to be well-thought out themselves if they are to have any chance of validating a given body of data.

Applying these validation processes to data that is strictly quantitative would be difficult enough. When applying them to a dataset that is in any significant degree a mixture of qualitative and quantitative elements, or data from disparate datasets over different spans of time, would compound the complexity and risk to the point that trusting the output borders on negligence.

And these layers of complexity all rest on the key assumption that the data in question are CLEAN in all critical aspects.

One is hard pressed to imagine a business executive acting on this "chain of validation-trust processes" if he or she knew how infused the entire process was with a high degree of uncertainty and significant risk.

It is not hard to imagine scenarios about all things data. Here are five related ones to consider for what they indicate about the pros and cons of hopping on the Bid Data Wagon Train.

Acme Electronics (AET- NYSE) is a major US-based engineering and design firm located in greater Los Angeles (annual sales in excess of $15B) that manufactures large flat screens (plasma display panels--PDPs) used in conference rooms to display all manner of information: from online internet content to corporate data dashboards and other reports featuring data rich KPIs, etc.

Scenario 1: A Data Scientist Candidate Interviews with HR and the Lead DBA at Acme Electronics

Sylvia, the Director of Human Capital Management (HCM): Tell me, Bill, what strengths do you offer Acme as a Data Scientist?

Bill Higgins: As you can see on my resume, I went to Cornell where I majored in Computer Science with a concentration in Computational Statistics.

Sylvia: You graduated in 2016, two years ago. I see from your resume that you have not yet worked as a Data Scientist full-time, which is kind of surprising since Data Scientists are one of the hottest job roles out there today. And believe me, people with your skill set and formal academic training are hard to find. Everyone seems to need a Data Scientist today, which includes Acme Electronics. So, your resume indicates you have yet to land a position. Have you been actively looking since you graduated?

Bill: I have looked but turned down several offers because we were far apart on salary and none of them were willing to help with my college loans. Also, they did not want the Data Scientist to basically be in charge of their Data. They were not all that clued in as to what the Data Scientist brings to the table. They were still in the mode of their executives making major decisions independently of what the data has to offer. They were just running the standard kinds of reports against the data, maybe doing a little in the way of standard dashboards, with some minor mining projects, but nothing too advanced or interesting to tell you the truth. So, in the meantime, I have been working at Starbucks but have been keeping up with the scientific literature. After attending two Data Analytics bootcamps, I did some consulting in data modeling on the side, which is listed in my resume.

Sally, DBA: Tell me, Bill, how would you go about building and managing a database that contains Big Data?

Bill: First, I would list all the factors that make for GIGO and address each of them in logical order.

Sally: A good approach. And have you done that in the real world, or only at Cornell?

Bill: Mostly at Cornell in hands-on-work at the data lab, but some for one of my part-time clients last year. They are still working on cleaning up their data, following the approach I gave them. Last time I heard from them, they were scrubbing away by revising their data definitions and updating the data dictionary.

Sylvia: Sally, I hope you're following all this.

Sally: I am, Sylvia. I eat, speak, and sleep data, you know.

Sylvia: Yes, I know you do. Now tell me, Bill, about yourself and why you want to join the team at Acme Electronics.

Scenario 2: A Working Session with the Data Team at Acme Electronics

The Situation: The team is in the "Protons Live Forever" huddle room.

Bill Higgins, the newly hired Data Scientist, is running the meeting. Sally Browne, the Lead DBA and her minions are also present.

The purpose of the meeting is to prepare the outline for a presentation that the CIO asked Bill and Sally to put together for the upcoming Board of Directors meeting.

Bill: Okay, what do we know for 100% sure about Acme's Big Data? Tell me, and I will write it on the board.

Sally: For 100% sure we know nothing other than it is ancient, big, and getting bigger by the nanosecond.

(Bill takes a seat)

Pete: You can say that again.

Juan: Amen to that, brother.

Sally: Pete, you have been here since we moved the data from on-premise to the Cloud. What can you tell Bill about how that went?

Pete: We moved it to the Cloud with much consulting assistance. Took us several months to get it all moved. It was moved as is, so what was in it all along went to the new platform. It is now managed by offshore teams for the most part. We did some cleanup beforehand, but nothing major. It was such a big job just to make all the steps needed for the move all into place. We had a narrow scope and limited budget, as I recall. James was the PM on that one, but I think he has left the company, or we could ask him for more details.

Sally: And what about the errors of late that marketing has reported to us, Pete?

Pete: Anomalies of one kind or another have been reported by marketing over the past five or so days. And yesterday by sales, finance, and supply chain. They had a handful of issues. I am guessing due to file upload files of new data. Or maybe from data entry errors. For missing data, one analyst in my group suggested maybe data leakage.

Sally: First I've heard of leakage.

Bill: We have check logs to show record counts. Can you get us the logs and a list of the specific errors reported over the last six months?

Pete: I can ask Martin to get that information for us, but he will need some time to round it up. Depends on the level of detail you are after.

Sally: We have asked for this before without getting much to go on.

Bill: Let's get what we can and then meet with business, so they can explain what is wrong, when they noticed it.

Sally: Sounds good.

Pete: Okay, I'll see Martin, but I think he is out sick today.

Bill: See him as soon as you can.

Pete: Hey, it's not the first time for me and Martin, so I know what to ask for and I know what he can get out of the business. Finance can be hard to work with, not to mention engineering.

Sally: Just do what you can with Martin, and if he is not able to get you what we need just let Bill and me know. We will go to the CIO.

Bill: As Pete has something for us to look at, we'll assess and come up with a plan.

Sally: Sounds good.

Bill: Thanks everyone for your time. Sally, please hang on a minute, okay?

After the team leaves the Huddle Room, Bill and Sally have the following exchange.

Bill: I know one task I must tackle is to figure out how to organize the data, but this looks like immediate issues to address ASAP.

Sally: We will have to loop in with the offshore provider and their DBAs for sure. They are 12-hours out of our workday.
Bill: What a mess we could have on our hands.
Sally: We need to tell the CIO that we have to figure out what the problems are before we present any plan to the Board.

Bill: Well, we have six weeks to figure it out and put together our Board power point.

Sally: Should be time enough.

Bill: Should be. Let's get a coffee and call the offshore data vendor.

Sally: Okay, sounds like a plan.

Bill: Sounds something like one, but still need your thinking on all this. Let's go get a coffee. I am buying.

Scenario 3: Conference Call with Acme's Client Executive for Data Storage in the Cloud

Bill: So, what you are telling me, Yvonne, is that we have to schedule at least a week out to get a copy of the entire data set; once it is available, we can then run diagnostics against it to identify the kind and extent of data issues, but we need to use your resources to run the diagnostics, is that right?

Yvonne: Right about all of that, Bill. It's in your Cloud Data contract. But just so we are all clear, you will have to take all of the production data, and that will mean *ad hoc* data storage fees while we are analyzing the data with you.

We will need a week to make a certified copy and another two weeks to stage and then analyze it and then make available to you our findings for your review and follow up. That fee will be around $25K or so. I will send you the Work Order today if you like, with the refined cost estimate.

Sally: What if we only take a representative sample of the data? That will cost less and will be faster to turn around, right?

Yvonne: Yes, it will cost less but I am afraid we will still take just as long to copy a sub-set of your production data and then analyze it. But I must advise against taking that approach.

Bill: Why is that, Yvonne? Isn't a representative sample of say 20 or so gigabytes sufficient to check for systemic corruption?

Yvonne: Because Acme has a mixed data set, something that many of our clients have, that's why. It got that way through mergers, acquisitions, and the like. This is especially true for Acme. You manufacture in the States, Germany, the Far East, even in Australia I believe. Your data is complicated by language, currency, not to mention by governing regulations that impact you as an international manufacturer and sales organization.

Bill: I assumed some mixture of data, some variety of data origins, but this sounds like years of diverse data infusion into Acme's native data set.

Sally: I am afraid that Yvonne is right. Bill, I thought you already were brought up to speed by the team and the CIO on these key facts. And you know Yvonne runs a Hadoop shop, right?

Bill: So, we are talking data from X sources, from foreign manufacturers, etc. And I have no preference for Hadoop over Spark, as long as they run the right analyzer tool set to give us the alerts and other data anomaly heads up, we need on likely cause and effect.

Yvonne: We always run those diagnostic tools, it's part of your maintenance fee. Azrot, your assigned team lead, will go over the Hadoop analytical tool set with you and your team, Bill, when you speak to him.

Bill: Anything else?

Yvonne: We have looked at partnering with MapR[78] and offering to our clients their concept of DevOps and using a "data fabric" that lets you work with disparate data sets like Acme's. They are good at anomaly detection. If you like, I will send you some YouTube links and then maybe arrange a meet up?

---

[78] MapR has many promotional and explanatory spots available on YouTube: here are three of many:
https://www.youtube.com/watch?v=VZMUVeZIYxQ; and also
https://www.youtube.com/user/maprtech; and
https://www.youtube.com/watch?v=qCgqD4_O5v4

Sally: Sure, send them, especially the link on anomaly detection.

Scenario 4: Inside the Acme Electronics Boardroom

Acme's Board meets twice a year, on the third Wednesday of the months of January and July. It is 10 AM PST in January and they are assembled in the Board Room, drinking coffee, munching pastries, checking their email on their phones and tablets.

On the PDP on the wall at the end of the large conference room table is the major topic for discussion by the Board at this meeting:

"Board to APPROVE OR DENY these two proposed courses of action by Acme's Executive Leadership Team:

1) **Acme's proposed plan to analyze its Big Data to determine via modeling scenarios the best steps to take across all manufacturing facilities in order to improve overall quality of product and reduction in supply chain, manufacturing, and distribution cost of the PDP product line manufactured in China and assembled in Vietnam.**

2) **Acme's proposed plan to analyze its Big Data via modeling to help senior management determine and validate the projected cost-benefits, potential profit margins, and market acceptance risks if Acme were to introduce a new product line of Digital Light Processing (PLP) Screens (to be manufactured and assembled in Brazil) for the South and North American corporate market sectors.**

Acme's data as of January 2018 is in excess of 200 terabytes[79] and growing fast; it is the result of every aspect of what Acme

---

[79] 1 TB = 1000000000000bytes = 1012bytes = 1000gigabytes

has accumulated in its Global SAP ERP system since its founding by Charles Ertzer, Ph.D., Cal Tech, Electrical Engineering, inventor, patent holder, major donor to the Republican Party nationwide. The data dates from 1983 and is a mixed dataset, consisting of data from various engineering, design, manufacturing, marketing, finance, sales, legal, state, US, and foreign government entities.

The Board of Directors is comprised of these individuals:

- Charles Ertzer, Jr., BA, Stanford, Marketing, Acme Chairman of the Board, CEO of Bakers Unlimited, an online retailer of bakery equipment for the home baker and small commercial bakeries
- Martha Smith, MBA, Oregon State, SVP Finance, Cal Bank
- Ed Martinez, BA, Pepperdine, Director of Outreach Programs, Southern District of Caltrans
- Abner Scruggs, JD, UCLA, SVP and Chief Legal Affairs Officer, Southern California Healthcare Association
- John Talmidge, BS, Physics, Princeton University, MBA, Harvard, CEO, Acme Electronics
- Gerome Goldner, MBA, Wharton, CFO, Acme Electronics
- Jimmy Acostamans, BA, Cal State, Northridge, President and CEO, Acostamans Industrial Electronics
- Peggy Browne, MBA, Syracuse, SVP Marketing and Sales, Teller's Global Electronics

The presentation to the Board will be made by Acme's newly hired Data Scientist, Bill Higgins, 25 (, Cornell, BS Computer Science. Arizona State University online MS, Computational Statistics); Sally Browne, Lead DBA, 35, (BS, Cal State, Irvine, Computer Science); and Randy Eckles, 52 (Cal State Poly, BS Mechanical Engineering, MS Computer Science, Stanford).

Key Consideration Points:

1. Will the presenters provide:
    a. all the steps that go into assessing the "health" of Acme's current Big Data?
        i. A realistic overview of the ongoing data cleansing and root cause error analysis of the sporadic incidence of spurious data that is experienced by Engineering, Finance, Marketing, and Sales; and the progress made to date, the tasks left to complete, and the timing when the cleansing and other remedies are completed by the Cloud Data Vendor's offshore data resource team.
        ii. The level of risk to proposed data mining and modeling that the current limited error assessment project poses, and is that risk level acceptable and within operating parameters that are acceptable based on industry-wide standards?
    b. what Big Data is, how it is mined, and how data models can be constructed and analyzed by Acme's Data Team?
    c. the pros and cons of Big Data mining, modeling, and the vagaries of reaching conclusions based on the assumptions that underlie the data mining models?
    d. how the Acme Data team will scrub clean all models of algorithmic bias?
    e. in ranked-order the various Risks inherent in this kind of Big Data analysis via modeling and analytics?

f. a timeline and high-level task steps to arrive at the answers to both questions before the Board?

g. An overview of the Acme Data Team's org chart, team roles, responsibilities, and qualifications, and a summary of the Project Manager's qualifications who has been selected to manage the project?

h. a breakout of the estimated costs for internal resources and external consulting experts who will be needed to conduct the mining and prepare the results for presentation to and approval by the Board at its next meeting?

Assume that Bill and Sally present via the standard show and tell all of the above in a very through and professional manner. Also assume that Randy says very little since he is not up to speed at all in the area of big data, modeling, so forth.

- What questions do you think the Board members will ask?
- Will the Board members have the requisite background to delve into the issues and ask the right questions to the extent needed to completely understand and challenge the key assumptions behind the proposal presentation?
- On a scale of 1-10, with 10 being the max, what level of TRUST and confidence do you think the Board will accord the presenters from Acme?
- Will the Board recommend after the meeting (and convey to the CEO, CFO, and CIO) that an outside data expert meet with Acme's Data Team and the Cloud Data Vendor to assess?

- o The Vendor's expertise in analyzing data error and its approach being used to determine the root causes of Acme's database errors;
  - o The Acme data team's qualifications and experience with Big Data model design, use, and analysis of results?
  - o The Acme data team's ability to understand the root cause analysis results presented by the Vendor data team, and to recommend best next steps to the Board?
- Will the Board give only a conditional approval to proceed as Acme management proposes without any of the double-checking first via an outside data expert?
- Will the Board, as it has in the past, put its trust in what is presented by Acme's technical resources (in this case, by Bill, Sally, and Randy) and approve the estimated $735K in capital expenditures to cover estimated consulting and travel costs of the resources tasked to conduct the data mining, modeling, and analytical predictive/assessment project?

Scenario 5: The Acme Electronics CEO Meets with his Data Evangelists in the Boardroom

The Acme Electronics Boardroom (note absence of pads, cells, and laps--and the scattered sheets of data on paper—and the ashtrays!)

In the Acme Boardroom we see the CEO (the mustachioed gent in foreground), the data engineer (behind the CEO), the CIO to his left, the data scientist (with the white square over his face—what does that portend?), the Director of Informatics (to the right of the CEO), and all the rest being your typical assortment of database administrators, business report managers, business analysts, and others who had something in IT to do with the data—but much less now that Acme's data resided in the Cloud and was the responsibility of a well-paid vendor of **international notoriety**.

Camera, lights, action.

The CEO passes out a bound document to each guru. The document contained all of the following text and graphics.

The CEO, John Talmidge, presides and conducts the meeting as follows, referring to the bound document in the hands of his people.

[Please put yourself in the seat of one of the data evangelists in attendance and read the following at your leisure. If you care to, send your own data guru answers to the author of this little book on data. His email is: whouze@gmail.com]

John's comments:

"First, thanks for being here to listen to (and read about) my concerns about our data.

As you might know, my formal schooling was a blend of two strains: physics and business. My undergraduate degree was in the former at Princeton, then I went on to Harvard Business. I have no background as such in the field of data science.

So, I consider that I have a non-technical background in all things Data.

First, I am going to give you my layman's view of how our data errors come about and why they remain in the system. You will see, I hope, why I have no sufficient level of trust in the validity and accuracy of our data. I could be wrong, of course, but I will need you to prove me wrong in the follow-up meetings I will hold with you after this kick-off session.

And I am asking you to put your heads together and present me with a clear plan and timeline to earn my trust in our data. Until that happens, I am not making any major business decisions that are based on what I see out of our data.

My Views, Opinions, and Questions

1. data of any kind (qualitative or quantitative) does not come about out of thin air. (Well, a physicist might say it

does, but we are not concerned with that today.) We create it in one way or another. We make it, capture it, give it structure, store it, display it, study it, and if all is well, believe in it.

2. as far as I know, we all make mistakes in everything we do. Despite trying our best to work in a mistake-free manner, we make them all the time, large and small, few and many. So, it follows for me that the data we created, entered into the system, stored, retrieved, and presented to be read, analyzed, understood, and acted upon in one way or another, for me, this entire series of data steps is by definition prone to error of one kind or another, or one magnitude or another.

3. I sum up my first two points with the well-known acronym, GIGO, or garbage in, garbage out. I believe GIGO is true more or less for all data in all computer systems of any size, complexity, age, and frequency of use and input of additional data elements on a routine basis and in high-volumes and complexity. That is us, if I am not mistaken.

4. errors exist in the data at all times and some are never discovered. Some are discovered. When they are, we try to get rid of them. But despite our best efforts to clean out the rotten data, we might not get it all out. And out very cleaning process might be flawed itself or might introduce more errors. What we think we have fixed might appear to be fixed at first, but later on, we find out we did not get all the cancerous cells out of the body of data. So along that long line of the "Chain of Data Custodial Events," humans and non-humans are the agents of mistakes, of viral infection, of systemic disease in the body of the data. Even a dataset containing one sentence, or ten random positive digits, or ten names and addresses and phone numbers can if

not entered with great precision, can contain errors. Multiply that a million-fold and you have systemic GIGO.

5. data errors made by us can have an impact ranging from the trivial and inconsequential to the most catastrophic in terms of impact on the health and well-being of our business, our employees, our customers, and let's not forget our investors and shareholders. And then there is hacking, security, all that kind of thing. This is especially critical for us since our datasets have grown exponentially over the past few years. We have made acquisitions and have brought that data into our master database; we have also kept them logically separate in many respects, but not in all respects; we have comingled, copied, truncated, and made one talk to another across cultures, languages, user groups, and over time spanning many years. The simple diagram below illustrates how A becomes B and B becomes C and A becomes C, and how all three datasets can share common data elements and therefore how all three can share one or more common and/or uncommon errors of many kinds in any one of them, in two of them, or across all three of them.

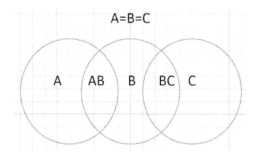

6. The CFO and I have read your proposals—and they are well done to be sure. In them, you make the case to spend a lot of our valuable capital on your well-

intentioned projects and programs; your aim is to mine our data, to build statistical models based on our data, to use our data in those models to predict which course of action, or series of actions, is most likely to be better for our bottom-line than alternative courses of action. Laudable goals, no doubt about that.

7. Let's assume that sake of this discussion that all of our data is pristine in every imaginable respect. That it is all there, is all totally correct, is free of all errors of all possible kinds made by any and all of the humans or machines or software programs that encountered the data in any way at all throughout the long chain of events in the life of a single datum.

8. And let's assume the CFO and I approve the proposals before us for mining, modeling, predicting, explaining, supporting, and substantiating in all possible ways the actions you propose to take with the data we own.

9. What does the data hold within its confines, within the databases we have, manage, and protect, what data are in there that can be manipulated by you in any number of ways such that it will reveal crucial facts, trends, discoveries, basic truths, general principles, rules, puzzles, riddles, anomalies, curiosities that once brought to light of day and placed before us in some presentable and understandable way, a report, a graph, a plot of data points, a set of statistical projections, a recommended course of one action over another— what will result that we have not already known in our day to day running of the business? What gems of unknown truth will the data yield? Has the data all along been a fount or a repository of knowledge? Have we ignored out of our ignorance of it what has been right before our us all this time? Has the data been our in any way a record of our past, our history? And if so, is

the past the keeper of the wisdom we need to know about in order to act in the future in ways that avoid the mistakes we made in the past? I believe it was George Santayana who said this, but much more eloquently than I have here.

10. So, help me understand the following:
    a. why I should approve proposed actions on a dataset that is not free of errors now and is likely to never be cured of all errors?
    b. why models and analysis that are based on and use our data will be produce results that are free of the same errors that plague the database in the first place?
    c. why the data holds valid information based on our past activities of all kinds that can be believed as a trustworthy set of executives, senior, and middle management recommendations for actions we should take in the future as we run the business? Is data the mythical Sphinx, the fount of knowledge and wisdom that is hidden but can be made available to us if we only ask it the right questions of it? Do our data hold truths waiting to be revealed to all who seek it if they only know how to find it?
    d. why the CFO's and my questions about our data and my reservations about your proposals that are based on our data are not a classic case of *reductio ad absurdum.*

Next, I want to pose some questions about data mining, modeling, and predictions

"I went to Quora and did some poking about, asking one thing and another to get my thoughts in order for our meeting today.

I came across a discussion about the "data science process" in Quora.[80] The graphic below is from a data science/statistics course taught at my alma mater:

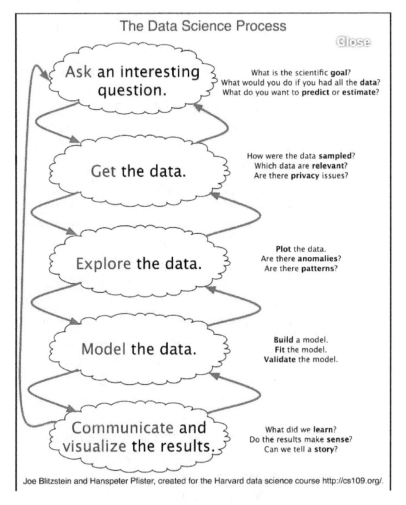

Joe Blitzstein and Hanspeter Pfister, created for the Harvard data science course http://cs109.org/.

Here are my questions about the process as depicted:

- Is the process dependent on a valid, error-free dataset?

80 https://www.quora.com/search?q=quantify+big+data

- Is the process based on a sample of the data, all of the data, and if on a sub-set of the total data, is that sub-set a valid representation of all of the data in the same class/type of data?

Next, I looked in Quora for information on the data mining process, since that figures prominently In your proposal to mine and model, then offer predictive outcomes for my consideration and possible follow up action on and implementation within the business:

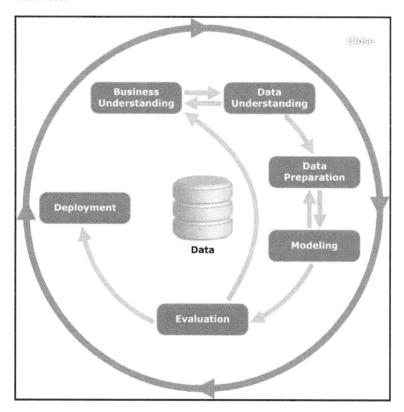

The data mining process[81]

You have probably heard that I am skeptical about data mining, modeling, predicting, all that sort of thinking that is all the vogue these days. But to be clear, here are some of my questions:

- There are layers of assumptions throughout this process. One big one, for example, is right at the top: business understanding. That is critical in my book.
- Even more important is the overall assumption that shouts out at me when I look at the data mining process as depicted by one person who placed it in Quora:
  - What about the integrity of the data that is shown at the center of the graphic? Was it an oversight to not put a label there, indicating that the dataset has been checked and verified as being sound in all respects?
  - If there is no effort to scrub, validate, and certify via the business, engineering, et al., and the vendors too, that the data is valid, what is the point of mining when the data is equal to what one finds at the bottom of your typical swamp in the Everglades?
  - Is the data scrubbed, validated, so forth in the data understanding step? In the data prep step? I am guessing it is not. That would mean cleaning up a fraction of the total and then on that small sample basing who knows what kind of wide conclusions? Talk about irresponsible extrapolation, even within the confines of standard logical inferences.

---

[81] https://www.quora.com/Are-there-any-thematic-frameworks-unifying-data-science-approaches-and-methods

○   What are we to make of all this?

Ladies and gentlemen, here are my layman's thoughts and questions on predictive data modeling based on big data:

- Which modeling toolset is suitable for our data, who makes that decision, and how is that model verified as being the appropriate one to use with our data? How reliable is that model? There are many competing and/or specialized modeling sets/programs and methodologies out there. Why are there so many?
- Is the number due to competing vendors pushing this or that? Or is the number due to sound scientific fact-based specification for one over another to meet:
  - ○   the conditions at hand
  - ○   the goal of the modeler
  - ○   the kind of data, the volume, the complexity
  - ○   the requirements of the business to see a specific kind of data presentation that only is possible if one uses model approach X instead of Y or Z?
- What tools are available to clean our data that is put into the data model toolset? Can we use only a clean sub-set as a sound basis from which to extrapolate? And what is the right amount of data that will be used in the modeling process?
- Will we use data from various time periods in our data life stream to handle fluctuations in whatever impacts our data by the day, week, month, year?"

Finally, here are some typical dashboards[82] I want you to review so we can discuss them and possibly come up with some answers to questions I have about them.

These dashboards focus on points in time in the areas of finance, supply chain, and project task status.

82

https://www.bing.com/images/search?&q=Executive+Dashboard&qft=+filterui:license-L2_L3_L4&FORM=IRFLTR

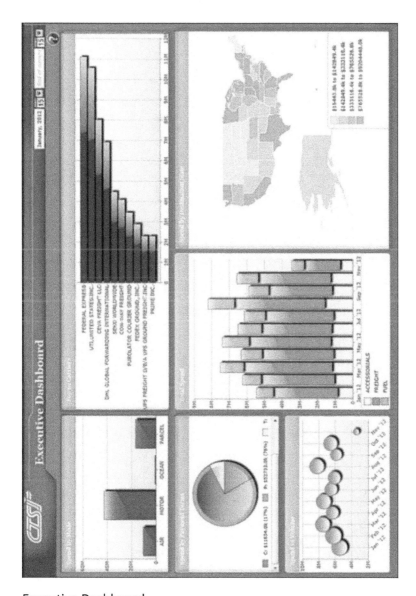

Executive Dashboard

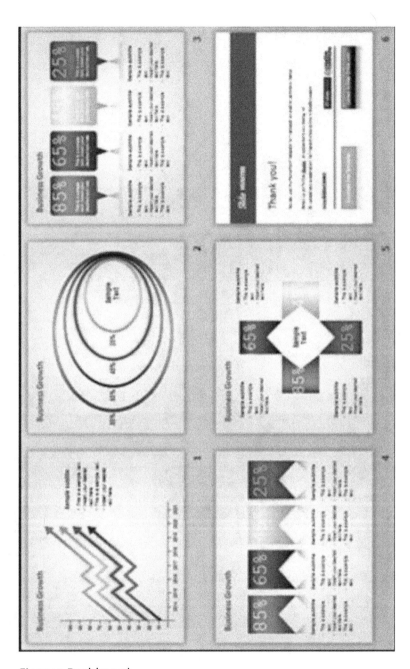

Finance Dashboard

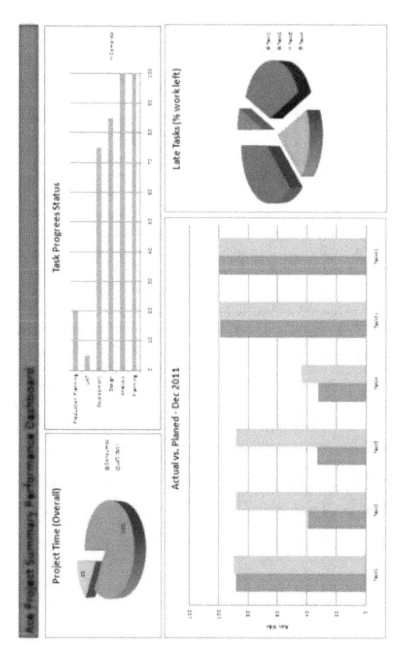

Project Status Dashboard

With these and similar ones in mind, I ask these basic questions:

1. How does a typical data dashboard convey anything that is actionable beyond the most basic interventions that a line manager can take?
2. Who will ensure that dashboard and other data-based reports are intelligible and understandable by those who request and/or receive them due to being on a distribution list?
3. Do we need to hold data interpretation classes across the business to ensure data output is used in the right way at the right time by the right people?
4. We often talk about "flipping the pyramid," that is giving middle managers the authority and tools they need to make decisions at their level which will keep the decision up and down the pyramid as close as possible to those who know what they are talking about because they live it day after day. But if the flipping involves empowering them with dashboards and other data output reports, do we need to determine first if they are getting the data they need, and second, if they understand it and how to act upon it? **This is key, in my view, to creating greater efficiencies by decentralizing decision-making up and down the pyramid.**
5. Please prepare a CEO-focused dashboard or a report for me that focuses on design engineering, or quality control, or manufacturing and assembly data. We are, after all, a maker of electronic displays that come out of engineering and QC. I need to see what the content is, what it means, and how I can use it—or not use it, and why not.
6. Do we need a dashboard, for example, that shows headcount gain/loss in departments across the business? What actionable purpose would that serve? Can't we call or email HR to find out if we want to

know? Would not a department manager know his or her headcount losses, gains, and needs without seeing a dashboard tally alert or pie chart or trend line on their desktop when they fire it up every morning?

7. Are dashboards at all meaningful for executives?
8. how can the dashboard present a cogent data "story" that can be read, understood, and then used as a sound basis upon which to formulate and put into action one or more tactical and/or strategic chain of events?
9. If the data dashboard is not meant to be used for tactical or strategic planning and execution purposes by executives, what are they good for? (One showing we are running out of a key component would trigger a buyer to issue a purchase order. But there are other ways, and less expensive ways, to handle that kind of operational necessity totally outside of costly dashboards, right? Consider Kanban and JIT supply chain inventory, for example.)

To close out my prepared remarks, I offer you the following brief overview of the distinctions that are to be made between **data, information, knowledge, and wisdom:**[83]

- Data, information, knowledge and wisdom are closely related concepts, but each has its own role in relation to the other, and each term has its own meaning
- According to a common view, data is collected and analyzed
- Data only becomes information suitable for making decisions once it has been analyzed in some fashion
- Knowledge is the understanding based on extensive experience dealing with information on a subject

---

[83] https://en.wikipedia.org/wiki/Data

- Wisdom complements and completes the series: "data," "information," and "knowledge" of increasingly abstract concepts
- Data is often assumed to be the least abstract concept, information the next least, and knowledge the most abstract. In this view, data becomes information by interpretation

Source materials to review before we meet again:

1. Big data: The next frontier for innovation, competition, and productivity McKinsey
   https://www.mckinsey.com/business-functions/digital-mckinsey/our-insights/big-data-the-next-frontier-for-innovation

2. **5 Essential Principles for Understanding Analytics**

   https://hbr.org/2015/10/5-essential-principles-for-understanding-nalytics?referral=03759&cm_vc=rr_item_page.bottom

3. **Prepare Your Organization to Capitalize on Predictive Analytics**

   https://www.sas.com/content/dam/SAS/en_us/doc/whitepaper2/hbr-capitalize-on-predictive-analytics-107427.pdf

4. **The Data Economy: Why do so many analytics projects fail? | Analytics Magazine**

   http://analytics-magazine.org/the-data-economy-why-do-so-many-analytics-projects-fail/

Thank you for your time and assistance in "all things data."

. I look forward to sharing and discussing our collected thoughts in the very near term.

Acme must approach its data with caution, of course, but also with some degree of optimism as to its potential value above and beyond the manner in which it has always been utilized over the years.

Talk to you soon,

John

DISCRETION IS THE BETTER PART OF VALOR
ERGO
THIS PAGE INTENTIONALLY LEFT BLANK

There is a wealth of literature available on the topic of the causes and preventions of data corruption in the Cloud.

Here are several key observations and findings gleaned from the literature (by no means an exhaustive review; that would take months to do a proper assessment).

1. "Understanding Real World Data Corruptions in Cloud Systems,"[84] by Peipei Wang, Daniel J. Dean, Xiaohui Gu, Department of Computer Science, North Carolina State University, Raleigh, North Carolina

This paper focused on "138 data corruption incidents reported in the bug repositories of four Hadoop projects."

The major causal agents identified were:

- hardware faults (e.g., memory errors, disk bit rot)
- software faults (e.g., software bugs)

Data corruption detection

On the topic of data corruption detection (built into the data management software/hardware schema), the study produced this telling and quite alarming graphic:

---

[84] http://dance.csc.ncsu.edu/papers/ic2e2015.pdf

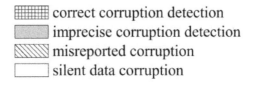

correct corruption detection
imprecise corruption detection
misreported corruption
silent data corruption

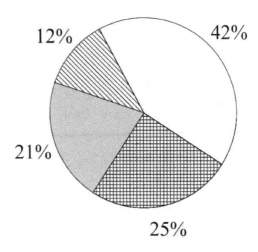

Fig. 2.   Different types of data corruption detection.

Key findings in the study were:

- Data corruption impact is not limited to data integrity
- Data corruption can be caused by various software bugs including both external and internal to HDFS
- Existing data corruption detection mechanisms are insufficient with both mis-detections and false alarms
- If corrupted blocks are not handled correctly, the data they store could be completely lost.
- Corrupted metadata prevents data from being accessed, which might cause wrong data deletion in some cases.

Now let's take a look at another article, this time stepping down from the Ivory Tower to a very short piece of some note on its own merits in **ZDNet.**

Robin Harris, writing for *Storage Bits,* March of 2012,[85] has some truly alarming information that should keep everyone up all night, sitting beside their terminals, hoping they receive no emails telling of disaster unfolding.

And by the by, don't assume that much progress has been made since 2012—that all in Cloud data land in 2018 is fine and dandy when it comes to massive data corruption, loss, financial disaster for clients who have entrusted their data to Cloud vendors.

Here are some key highlights from Harris's piece:

"In a recent post Amazon Web Services Vice President and Distinguished Engineer James Hamilton - formerly of Microsoft - writes about his experience with errors on high-scale systems.

Harris recounts Hamilton's experience as follows:

- **Hardware, software and firmware** all introduce errors. ". . . absolutely nobody and nothing can be trusted."
- **More error detection is always better**. Every time he's added more, he's been ". . . amazed at the frequency the error correction code fired."
- **Corruption is everywhere**. In one case he found latent data corruption on customer disks that was so bad that customers thought the software was buggy while the real problem was on-disk.
- **You absolutely need ECC on servers**. And, he concludes ". . . ECC memory should be part of all client systems."

---

[85] http://www.zdnet.com/article/data-corruption-at-massive-scale

(Note: ECC is "error-correcting code")

Not to put too fine a gloom and doom point on it, Harris gives this concluding assessment by Hamilton:

"corruption exists at every level of the storage, network, and compute stack. File systems, drivers, disks, NICs, switches, DRAM and more."

Finally, here is what Microsoft has to say about data corruption in Microsoft Office 365, which resides in the Cloud.

Robert Mazoli, et al. writes 8/20/2018 the following in a piece titled "Dealing with Data Corruption in Office 365"[86] about the challenges Cloud data vendors face:

"One of the challenging aspects of running a large-scale cloud service is how to handle data corruption, given the large volume of data and independent systems. Data corruption can be caused by:

- Application or infrastructure bugs, corrupting some or all of the application state
- Hardware issues that result in lost data or an inability to read data
- Human operational errors
- Malicious hackers and disgruntled employees
- Incidents in external services that result in some loss of data"

He offers these words of comfort to those who fear that their data, once up in the Office 365 Cloud, will be lost forever:

---

[86] https://docs.microsoft.com/en-us/office365/securitycompliance/office-365-dealing-with-data-corruption

"Microsoft has built into Office 365 protection mechanisms to prevent corruption from happening, as well as systems and processes that enable us to recover data if it does. **Checks and processes exist within the various stages of the engineering release process to increase resiliency against data corruption**, including:

- System Design
- Code organization and structure
- Code review
- Unit tests, integration tests, and system tests
- Trip wires tests/gates

(emphasis added)

Then the authors offer this reassuring bit of verbiage about data center fail-over and redundancy and recovery, all meant to ensure the Enterprise that no data will be lost, and one center downfall will immediately be counteracted by bringing a duplicate dataset at another physical datacenter location:

"Within Office 365 production environments, peer replication between datacenters **ensures that there are always multiple live copies of any data**. Standard images and scripts are used to recover lost servers, and replicated data is used to restore customer data." (emphasis added)

Incidence of Data failure in Cloud

One observation is that the reporting of Cloud disasters seems to be much easier to find 5 or 10 years back, but not very much from 2015 to current time. One reason might well be there have been major improvements in detection and correction of errors that could lead to disaster.

But how likely is this to be the case? Has the technology gotten all that much better since the advent of the Cloud for running

ERP apps and storage of data that those apps use and generate in the course of doing business?

Are the Cloud vendors hiring only the best talent and training them in all the latest methodologies and intervention protocols that head off any hint of data corruption and loss well before the chain of events gets started?

Is the data error detection software so good now, and across all aspects of the hardware, network, storage mechanisms, backup routines, etc. that humans are now largely out of the management of Cloud data storage and retrieval, and thus the better software and hardware make large scale silent data loss nearly impossible?

Data is Everything, is Everywhere, is Evermore

- Data is everywhere, all the time, and is increasing in magnitude and possibly in complexity as well
- Data is not going anywhere, it is here to stay
- Like it or not, we are in the primordial and infinite data swamp and there is no easy way out—even if you wanted to find the public boat ramp where you put in to that nice looking bayou
- Some data are more useful and reliable than others
- Data is seductive, mind-numbing, but also appealing to the human intellect
- Humans enjoy thinking about data, manipulating data, creating schemas of all sorts about how to capture, compare, manage, govern, and make the best possible use of data
- Humans think data is a pathway to prosperity if it is only mined correctly
- Humans will try all manner of ways to use data to predict the future based on data from the past and near-time-present
- The human brain enjoys thinking about, classifying, manipulating, and pondering the meaning of and many challenges presented by data
- It is the nature of the human brain to go anywhere and think about anything, even replacing itself with AI

ERP System Data

- ERP systems have been around since the days of MRP I
- ERP data is relatively stable and understandable
- More than not, the Enterprise can make good use of ERP system data in the areas of:
  - Supply chain demand planning

- o Inventory management
- o Production planning
- o Financial regulatory reporting, taxation compliance, budget consumption, bottom-line tally for the Annual Report
- o Routine HR records keeping for staff metrics and benefit enrollment elections, etc.
- o Quality control metrics and record keeping showing evidence of failures and corrective action taken when, how, and by whom
- o Design engineering, CADCAM, etc.
- o Document scanning and retention

ERP System Data Report Output

- Standard reports showing historical and near-time data can be generated out of the ERP and other systems for the above ERP operational areas
- Dashboard information showing ERP system data trends and measurements of operational performance are nice but not really essential.
- They are historical static reports, check points in time past showing the count of this or that event or operation over some defined period of time.
- ERP reports are usually understandable if formatted correctly; they can demand intervention by the user, but usually they do not, or they ask for action, but the user does not understand them or what action to take if they do understand what the data story is all about.
- They are usually just informative output, not a call to take up arms.
- Most users ask for business reports in their area of Enterprise operations, get them in soft or paper form, or both; some read them routinely, but many never read them routinely, if at all.

Executives Beware

- The data industry's legions of **01110111 01101111 01101100 01110110 01100101 01110010 01101001 01101110 01100101 01110011 00100000 01101001 01101110 00100000 01110100 01101000 01100101 00100000 01100111 01110101 01101001 01110011 01100101 00100000 01101111 01100110 00100000 01010011 01101001 01110010 01100101 01101110 01110011** will consume much money, time, and human resource energy if Executives let them in the door.
- Executives become mere extensions of the Internet of Things if they agree to have data pushed out night and day to their watches, cell phones, tablets, or laptops.
- Data deprives Executives of the time they need to think, analyze, plan, share ideas with their peers.
- The only critical reports Executives need to pay attention to are the financial reports. All the rest is clutter and noise.
- Executives need to attend an impartial bootcamp of their own just to learn enough about the following to avoid making mistakes; or because they are prone to trust what subordinates (CIO?) tell them; or because they think they should take data to heart because the competition is awash in it day and night and claims their bottom-line is enriched by making data the most important thing to come down the pike. CEOs, CFOs, CIOs, VPs of HR and Operations, all need to know more about:
  - Big Data
  - Data Mining
  - Data Modeling
  - Predictive Analytics
  - Data Analytics
  - Data Corruption

141

- o Success and failure stories from Executives
- o Where the data industry is headed

CIO, Data Officer, Data Scientist, Data Engineer, other Data Gurus in the Enterprise

- Attend the Data Seminars for Executives with your Executives
- Ask Data Vendors the hard and challenging questions
- Advocate for the view that at least 99% of all Enterprise data is the transactional record of doing business, is the digitized recording of business history, is from the past, belongs in the past, **and is therefore not actionable**
- Learn all you can about the following:
    - o Preventing and detecting hacking into your data
    - o Preventing data theft by internal and external sources
    - o Ensuring data security if it is on-premise, in the Cloud, or in both domains (i.e., encrypted data in flight and at rest, so forth)
    - o Tools that can help detect data anomalies
    - o Tools that can help you establish proper data definitions, dictionaries, etc.
    - o Tools that can help cleanse your data and keep it clean
    - o Ways to educate the users of data reports across the Enterprise so they understand the basics of reports, what they mean, do not mean, and when they should raise the alarm if they see something that is out of the ordinary (new, missing, greater values/lesser values, so forth)
    - o Ensuring that your data vendor(s) who mind your Cloud data are up to snuff in all respects

- o Look at the cost of data from all perspectives and propose to senior management ways to reduce cost and cut out unnecessary data-related processes, methods, modeling, and the like because they do not contribute in a positive manner to enhancing the bottom-line
- o Put together in-house data seminars and workshops that impart greater understanding about the nature and use of data in your business; invite the Executives to attend; also, your data vendors, who should present but not sell their products

Biometrics

- Live in woods along the mid-coast of Maine -- with Mainer wife and English Springer
- *Slowly* reading the **Great Books**
  - Presently reading (again after some 30 years) **The Brothers Karamazov**
- Retired after 20+ years of consulting and managing various projects in ERP
- Checkered work history (academic, oil patch, cabinetmaker, custom home builder)
- Former professor in CA, NY, SD, MD
  - Literature
  - Philosophy
  - Professional writing
  - Expository writing
- Co-author of books on the Kaypro computer and its bundled software:
  - **The Kaypro - Plain and Simple**
  - **Kaypro Word Processing**
- Author of several books available from Amazon (paperback and Kindle):
  - **Survival**
  - **Poems to be Determined**
  - **Cogito ergo non opus est machina: I think therefore do not need a machine**
  - **DATA (The Primordial and Infinite Swamp)**
- Vietnam veteran, USMC
- Ph.D., Syracuse University
  - Joseph Conrad
- Member of Maine Mensa

- 1962 – Turkey: "The Future of Data Analysis"
- 1974 - Peter Nauru: "Concise Survey of Computer Methods"
- 1989 - Gregory Piatetsky-Shapiro: the first "Knowledge Discovery in Databases (KDD)" workshop
- September 1994: *BusinessWeek* publishes a cover story on "Database Marketing"
- 1996 - International Federation of Classification Societies (IFCS) meet in Kobe, Japan . . . the term "data science" is included in the title of the conference ("Data science, classification, and related methods")
- 1996 - Usama Fayyad, Gregory Piatetsky-Shapiro, and Padhraic Smyth publish "From Data Mining to Knowledge Discovery in Databases"
- 1997 -- Professor C. F. Jeff Wu, Georgia Tech, "calls for statistics to be renamed data science and statisticians to be renamed data scientists"
- 1997 -- The journal *Data Mining and Knowledge Discovery* launched
- December 1999 -- Jacob Zahavi in "Mining Data for Nuggets of Knowledge" stresses big data in terms of scalability, data model building, and developing special data mining tools
- 2001 -- William S. Cleveland publishes "Data Science: An Action Plan for Expanding the Technical Areas of the Field of Statistics"
- 2001 -- Leo Breiman publishes "Statistical Modeling: The Two Cultures". He points out that it is important ". . . to move away from exclusive dependence on data models and adopt a more diverse set of tools."

- April 2002 -- "Launch of *Data Science Journal*, publishing papers on "the management of data and databases in Science and Technology"
- January 2003 -- Launch of *Journal of Data Science*
- May 2005 -- Thomas H. Davenport, Don Cohen, and Al Jacobson publish "Competing on Analytics," a report that points out this key notion: **"the emergence of a new form of competition based on the extensive use of analytics, data, and fact-based decision making... Instead of competing on traditional factors, companies are beginning to employ statistical and quantitative analysis and predictive modeling as primary elements of competition."** (emphasis added) [It is noteworthy that this report marks, in my view, the abandonment of empirical science for the "new science" that I argue lives in the data swamp. The authors champion "predictive modeling as the primary elements of competition."]
- September 2005 -- The National Science Board publishes "Long-lived Digital Data Collections: Enabling Research and Education in the 21st Century." The report espouses the importance of establishing a firm career path for data scientists.
- 2007 -- The Research Center for Dataology and Data Science is established at Fudan University, Shanghai, China
- July 2008 -- The JISC publishes the final report, stressing the critical need to promote the role and career of data scientists to work in the research community
- January 2009 – "Harnessing the Power of Digital Data for Science and Society" is published
- March 2009 -- Kirk D. Borne and other astrophysicists submit a paper titled "The Revolution in Astronomy Education: Data Science for the Masses

- May 2009 -- Mike Driscoll writes in "The Three Sexy Skills of Data Geeks" that data scientists are much in demand
- June 2009 -- Nathan Yau in "Rise of the Data Scientist" touts how this new breed of scientist can "do it all," who can ". . . **extract information from large datasets and then present something of use to non-data experts . . ..**" (emphasis added) [Again, this publication and others like it no doubt present, in my view, the notion that the data scientist will be the magician, the transformer of the opaque, the murky, and the mysterious data to reveal the hidden meaning, to present it in such a manner that the decision makers in key management positions across the Enterprise as well as government, military, health sciences, and R&D will grasp the meaning of what is presented; furthermore, they will empowered to formulate sound tactical and strategic plans, to make decisions that they otherwise might not be able to make, or might eventually make but not until they had stumbled about as blind men who cannot see the data right in front of their faces.]
- June 2009 -- Troy Sadkowsky creates the data scientists' group on LinkedIn
- February 2010 – Kenneth Cukier writes in The Economist Special Report" Data, Data Everywhere ":" ... **a new kind of professional has emerged, the data scientist, who combines the skills of software programmer, statistician and storyteller/artist to extract the nuggets of gold hidden under mountains of data**." ⚠ (emphasis and warning added) [Same response applies here as given immediately above.]
- June 2010 -- in "What is Data Science?" Mike Loukides extolls the manifold wonders and virtues of the data scientist: ". . . can tackle all aspects of a problem, from

initial data collection and data conditioning to drawing conclusions." [No comment needed, same as before.]

- September 2010 -- Hilary Mason and Chris Wiggins write in "A Taxonomy of Data Science" that "Data science is clearly a blend of the hackers' arts... statistics and machine learning... and the expertise in mathematics and the domain of the data for the analysis to be interpretable... **It requires creative decisions and open-mindedness in a scientific context."** ⚠ (emphasis and warning added) [Is this touting empiricism, marketing, or artistic renderings of bland and entangled layers of data into a beautiful story book full of easily understood and pleasing pictures added to embellish the storyteller's text?]
- September 2010 -- Drew Conway writes in "The Data Science Venn Diagram": "...one needs to learn a lot as they aspire to become a fully competent data scientist."
- May 2011 -- Pete Warden writes in "Why the term 'data science' is flawed but useful"
- May 2011 -- David Smith writes in "'Data Science': What's in a name?": "The terms 'Data Science' and 'Data Scientist' have only been in common usage for a little over a year, but they've really taken off since then: many companies are now hiring for 'data scientists', and entire conferences are run under the name of 'data science'.
- June 2011 -- Matthew J. Graham says: "We need to understand what rules [data] obeys, how it is symbolized and communicated and what its relationship to physical space and time is."
- September 2011 -- Harlan Harris writes in "Data Science, Moore's Law, and Moneyball": "'Data Science' is defined as what 'Data Scientists' do. . .. **In my conversations with people, it seems that people who**

consider themselves Data Scientists typically have eclectic career paths, that might in some ways seem not to make much sense." ⚠️ (emphasis and warning added)

www.ingramcontent.com/pod-product-compliance
Lightning Source LLC
LaVergne TN
LVHW051344050326
832903LV00031B/3737